Keto Bread Machine Cookbook #2020

This Includes: Keto Machine Cookbook + Bread

Simple, Cheap and Delicious Homemade Ketogenic Bread Recipes That Will Make your Life Easier

Katie Simmons

Table of contents

Keto Bread Machine Cookbook

Delicious, Mouth-Watering and Fat-Burning Keto Bread Recipes for Your Bread Machine

Katie Simmons

Text Copyright ©

Legal & Disclaimer

The information contained in this book and its contents is not designed to replace or take the place of any form of medical or professional advice; and is not meant to replace the need for independent medical, financial, legal or other professional advice or services, as may be required. The content and information in this book has been provided for educational and entertainment purposes only.

The content and information contained in this book has been compiled from sources deemed reliable, and it is accurate to the best of the Author's knowledge, information and belief. However, the Author cannot guarantee its accuracy and validity and cannot be held liable for any errors and/or omissions. Further, changes are periodically made to this book as and when needed. Where appropriate and/or necessary, you must consult a professional (including but not limited to your doctor, attorney, financial advisor or such other professional advisor) before using any of the suggested remedies, techniques, or information in this book.

Upon using the contents and information contained in this book, you agree to hold harmless the Author from and against any damages, costs, and expenses, including any legal fees potentially resulting from the application of any of the information provided by this book. This disclaimer applies to any loss, damages or injury caused by the use and application, whether directly or indirectly, of any advice or information presented, whether for breach of contract, tort, negligence, personal injury, criminal intent, or under any other cause of action.

You agree to accept all risks of using the information presented inside this book.

You agree that by continuing to read this book, where appropriate and/or necessary, you shall consult a professional (including but not limited to your doctor, attorney, or financial advisor or such other advisor as needed) before using any of the suggested remedies, techniques, or information in this book.

Introduction

Okay, how does one not love bread? You can be on a diet, you can avoid carbs, you can be on all of that, but we are sure you there is not a single person who does not appreciate bread. The link between humans and bread as food is mystical. As our first baked food, bread has been a part of our history since the beginning of time. Bread even played a role in the Bible and is incorporated into many holy ceremonies across the globe. So, who does not like bread'?

Hot golden crescent roll, freshly baked breakfast buns, fragrant cake for the tea time and delicious pie to go with the morning coffee - all of that can be cooked with a bread machine in mere minutes and with minimum effort of yours. Moreover, these tasty and healthy baked goods can be done with the simplest and common ingredients. The only particular thing you'll need to add is your love and creativity!

In today's society we all have tight schedules to keep up with. Most days, we barely have the time to make our own breakfast, lunch, and dinner. Because of this, we end up eating quick, expensive, and unhealthy connivance food. If you want to lose or manage your weight, binge-eating on junk and fatty foods is going to do the exact opposite, not to mention fill your body with chemicals and bad fats. This is why you need something that allows you to eat healthy, and at the same time, allows you to keep up with your very hectic schedule. This is when you need a bread machine and an excellent recipe to start you off. If you love your bread, this is the best book for you.

Even if you are not good at using modern appliances, leave your worries behind because bread machines have straightforward and user-friendly controls - using them is fun and pleasure! Along with making fresh bread, they can also make and knead any kind of dough, bake ready-to-use dough and even make some jam to go with the pastry! When you get to know this easy-to-use device, it will become a truly essential and irreplaceable help in your kitchen.

This recipe book is full of ketogenic bread recipes that will help curb your carb cravings. This book contains bread machine recipes divided into categories to make it easy for you. The recipes also have nutritional information to guide you on the amount of nutrients that you take into your body.

Start reading, and you will get into the world of keto bread machine baking. This book contains amazingly delicious keto bread maker recipes that are both easy to make and good for you.

Chapter 1: Keto bread and bread machines

What is Keto Bread?

Keto bread is a bread with very small amounts of gluten, sugar, and carbs. The best thing about the keto bread is that you can eat as much as you are able to without worrying about adding weight or sugar spikes. The flours that make the keto bread do not have the ordinary carbs present in other flours like wheat.

Coconut flour almond flour are the most common alternatives to grain flour used to make low carb breads. However, some people are allergic to almonds and in such cases, they can only use coconut flour.

Bread Machine

A bread machine, also known as the bread maker, a type of appliance that turns ingredients into baked bread. It comes with a bread pan at the bottom which looks like paddles in a pizza oven. The bread machine is often controlled by a display panel.

The first bread maker was founded in Japan in 1986 by Panasonic. The purpose of this machine was to train the head bakers to knead bread. As it was industrialized, more companies started creating their own version of the bread machine. Some added a cooling fan at the bottom to allow the machine to cool off after use. Not too long after, it became famous in the United States, Europe, and Australia.

The bread machine is an all-in-one appliance. It takes the guess work out of making bread by mixing, kneading, proving, and baking the dough. Usually, the bread machine takes a few hours to make a loaf.

Once done, the pan is removed from within the bread-maker, which leaves a small hole from the rod where the paddle is attached. Do not be put off by the odd shape of the bread from the machine. It is normal to produce vertical, square, or cylindrical loaves, which is very different from commercialized loaves.

The bread machine is considerably smaller in size than the standard oven. And the usage is defined by the capacity of the bread machine itself. In most cases, the bread machine can accommodate up to 1.5 pounds, or 700 grams of dough. There are also bread machines that can accommodate up to 900 grams of dough.

The typical bread maker comes with a built-in timer to control the start and end of the bread-making process. Most machines have a delayed start option, this allows the bread to start baking even when you are asleep or at work, meaning you'll be greeted by a fresh loaf.

Homemade bread tends to go stale faster than commercial bread as it does not contain any preservatives. There is a natural way to preserve your bread and it includes using a natural leaven and a pre-ferment in the bread machine. The reason behind this is that it contains a form of lactobacilli. The yeast is responsible for the flavor and the rising of the dough. The lactic acid is responsible for the preservation of the bread.

Benefits of Bread Machines

The main reason you will love your bread machine is the incredible variety of loaves you can create and enjoy without spending hours in the kitchen. There is something satisfying about popping out fragrant, fresh bread from the bucket knowing you made it yourself. However, here are some other reasons your bread machine will quickly become your favorite kitchen appliance:

Saves power.

Think about how warm your kitchen gets when you bake anything in the oven, especially during the summer months. Escaping heat is money out of your pocket, and even if you have a very well-insulated oven, it still costs more to run an oven than a bread machine. The power usage of a standard bread machine is thought to be about the same as or less than a coffeemaker, about 9 kilowatt-hours for 15 hours a month.

Set it and forget it.

You have time to do other tasks, run errands, or make the rest of a big meal without supervising the bread in the machine. Traditional bread making is more hands-on and requires a significant amount of time.

Cleanup is a breeze.

If you have ever made bread without a machine, you will be familiar with the dirty bowls, flour mess from kneading the dough, and washing up the pans or baking sheets. With the bread machine, you just dump the ingredients in and wash a couple measuring cups and spoons. Plus, bread machine buckets wipe off easily after the loaf is out.

Control over ingredients.

Knowing exactly what is in the food you set on the table is reassuring, especially if you have someone in the family with allergies or food issues. The ingredients you buy are completely under your control, so there are no unrecognizable ingredients in the finished loaf.

Saves money.

Almost all the ingredients you put into bread can be bought in bulk, which is the best way to save money.

Factors to Consider when Buying a Bread Machine

If you have already had your bread machine, there is no other choice besides maximizing its functions. However, if you haven't bought one, perhaps several points below can be a consideration in making a choice.

The Warranty

There is always a risk while operating the bread machine. You have to ensure that the brand you choose provides an after-sales service with free or cheap cost.

The Bread Machine Features

Almost all bread machines have the same menu setting. However, if it is possible, you can get the one with special features, for examples "Gluten-Free", "Dough" or "Fruits/Nuts" setting.

The Delay Timer

The delay timer is needed so that you can adjust the time when the bread should be done. The feature possibly you to enjoy warm fresh bread at the right moment.

The "Keep Warm" menu setting

The "Keep Warm" menu setting will automatically take care of the bread if you miss the schedule.

The Bread Size Option

The number of family members and the estimated amount of bread you need should determine the bread machine you are going to buy. Some bread machines are completed with three bread size options— 1 lb., 1-½ lbs., and 2 lbs.

The Viewing Window

The viewing window enables you to check the bread making process periodically.

The Bread Tin Shape

Most bread machines offer rectangular bread tin. Several bread machines serve round or square bread tin. You can choose it according to your desire.

The Bread Machine Size

The bread machine should be fit with your kitchen. If you don't have enough space in your kitchen, at least you have to manage where you are going to store the bread machine.

Those are several considerations before you buy your bread machine. Price is still a big consideration. However, thinking about quality over price is also important. Moreover, a bread machine is a smart and magical kitchen appliance. Having a bread machine is like hiring a professional baker.

Happy baking good people! Pick your favorite recipe and bake your bread in your bread machine.

Health benefits of a ketogenic diet.

Research has shown the ketogenic diet to be a great way to lose weight. That's cool and all, but losing weight shouldn't be the only thing you seek with a diet. You should have more energy, and better indications of health such as lower cholesterol. Starting a ketogenic diet can provide you with some amazing health benefits in addition to losing weight:

Prevention of diabetes: Diabetes is essentially an impaired function of insulin. Studies have shown the ketogenic diet to be able to improve insulin sensitivity. The higher your insulin sensitivity levels are, the less insulin your body will require to lower blood glucose levels back to normal. As you learned in the previous chapter, your body doesn't burn fat when insulin levels are high. Therefore, it's important to improve insulin sensitivity levels to help better regulate blood glucose levels.

Lower Risk for Heart disease: Heart disease is one of the leading causes of death in the United States, and it includes many risk factors such as cholesterol levels, body fat, blood sugar, and blood pressure. The ketogenic diet can help to improve these risk factors, thus lowering the risk for heart disease.

Getting rid of acne: Another cool side benefit is that it can help get rid of acne if you struggle with breakouts regularly. The ketogenic diet will help to lower insulin levels by eating less processed foods and sugar, which can help prevent acne.

Cancer treatment: The ketogenic diet is currently being used to treat several different types of cancer, and it can slow tumor growth. Of course, more research needs to be done for conclusive evidence.

Increase HDL cholesterol levels: There are two different kinds of cholesterol—HDL, which stands for high-density lipoproteins and

LDL, which stands for low-density lipoproteins. Your HDL is your good cholesterol that you want to increase because it's responsible for carrying cholesterol to the liver where it can then be excreted or reused. LDL's on the other hand, are bad cholesterol, and are responsible for carrying cholesterol away from the liver and into the body. Research shows one of the best ways to increase your HDL levels are to increase your fat intake. You'll easily be able to achieve that with the standard ketogenic protocol of 75% of your calories coming from fat.

Lower blood pressure: Lowering your carbohydrate intake has been shown to decrease hypertension. Having higher blood pressure increases your risk for developing diseases such as heart disease and stroke.

Decrease triglyceride levels: Triglycerides are a fat molecule. It might sound counter-intuitive that increasing your fat intake would decrease the amount of triglycerides in the blood, but it really does. This occurs because carbs are one of the biggest contributors to increasing triglycerides. Therefore, by decreasing carb intake, you'll decrease the amount of triglycerides in your blood.

More weight loss than a typical diet: Studies have shown that people who restrict calories on a low-carb diet lose more weight, and lose weight faster than individuals restricting calories on a low-fat diet. The main reason for this is because low-carb diets lower insulin levels, which will cause the body to get rid of excess sodium within the first few weeks of starting the diet.

A positive way to lose your appetite: When you go on a diet and restrict your calories, you start to feel hungry. If your feelings of hunger start to get out of control, you're more likely to quit and give up on your diet—and obviously if you quit and go back to your old habits, you have no chance of losing weight and improving your health. Luckily, eating a low-carb diet has been shown to decrease appetite. This is critical because it'll allow you to lower your overall caloric intake without having to worry about getting extra hungry.

Improves Digestion: The ketogenic diet contains low carbs, low grains, and low sugars, which can significantly improve your digestion. When you consume carbs and sugars on a regular basis, it can result in gas, bloating, stomach pains, and constipation. Reducing sugars and carbohydrates in your diet can restore your digestive system.

Increases Energy: A ketogenic diet can increase energy levels in multiple ways. It increases the mitochondrial function, and at the same time decreases the harmful radicals inside your body, thus making you feel more energetic and revitalized.

Improves Mental Health: The ketone bodies released when following ketogenic diet are directly connected to mental health. Research has shown that increased ketone levels can lead to stabilization of neurotransmitters, like dopamine and serotonin. This stabilization helps fight mood swings, depression, and other psychological issues.

Chapter 2: Ingredients And Tools Used

Knowing the wonders of the bread machine, every day may become the right day for baking bread. Below is the list of easy-to-store ingredients that you will need for making bread.

Flour

Flour is the main ingredient for making bread. The standard recipe in this book uses bread flour. However, other types of flour can also be used in making bread, such as rye, whole wheat, oats, soy, and many more options of flour. Additional information to be paid attention is that bread flour or white bread flour contains the most gluten and will result in more dense bread. On the other hand, some types of flour like corn flour or rice flour contain no gluten. So, if you want to get a decent rise of bread, you have to add a small amount of white bread flour.

Yeast

Yeast has a crucial role in the bread making process. It is the key ingredient to make the dough rise well resulting in the smooth and elastic dough. The best yeast suggested for bread machines is bread machine yeast. However, you can also use active dry yeast.

Liquids

The liquid is important in making bread since it activates the yeast and blends with flour to make a more elastic dough. Water may be the most common liquid used in making bread. However, to enhance the texture or flavor, some other liquid ingredients like milk, buttermilk, juice, or cream can also be used in making bread. The only thing to be paid attention is the temperature of the liquid that should be warm. If the liquid is too cool, it will stop the yeast action, while if it is too hot, the liquid will destroy the yeast.

Sweetener

Sugar is the common sweetener used for making bread, although other sweeteners like molasses, honey, jams, maple syrup, corn syrup, or brown sugar are also fine. Sugar is food for the yeast. However, giving too much sugar can inhibit gluten production. Unless you are going to add more gluten to the recipe—in the form of gluten flour, it is recommended to use a maximum of two tablespoons of sugar for every cup of flour. Besides having a role for the yeast, sugar also helps in giving a sweet flavor to the bread, browning the bread, and also tenderize the bread.

Salt

Salt slows the rising time of the bread and gives the dough more time to develop the flavor. For the best result, it is highly recommended not to omit salt for any yeast bread recipes.

Eggs

Eggs are a leavening agent that helps the dough to rise well. Besides, eggs enhance the protein content, flavor, and color of the bread. Also, the eggs make the bread crust tenderer.

Fats

Fat, which is involved in the bread making process will inhibit the gluten so that it will not rise as high as the bread without any fats. The good thing about fats—especially olive oil and butter, they enrich the flavor, tenderize the texture, and extend the life of the bread.

The ingredients listed above are only the basic ingredients needed for making bread. You can always follow your creativity by adding some herbs and spices to enhance the taste and the appearance of the bread. All you have to pay attention is that the crucial step in making bread using a bread machine is measuring the ingredients accurately. For the best result, it is recommended to use a digital scale, liquid measuring cups, dry measuring cups, and measuring spoons with an accurate number.

Tools Used

Pastry brush

Basting brush or pastry brush looks similar to a paintbrush. It is made of nylon or plastic fiber. It is used to spread glaze, oil, or butter on food.

Blender

It is an essential kitchen appliance used to emulsify, puree, or mix food. It comes with a blender jar designed with a rotating blade made of metal. The jar is powered by a motor.

Kitchen scale

A kitchen scale is a must-have kitchen tool. Preparing certain types of food without one is practically impossible. Yes, there are cups, but when it comes to dough-based meals, a kitchen scale is necessary equipment. The best example is bread, which is hard to make without a kitchen scale. The reason behind it is because flour is a compressible, and measurement in cups will sometimes just not be accurate. To get your bread dough perfect, we suggest you use kitchen scales. You can find classic and digital ones, but for the best accuracy, choose digital scales. They are so much easier to use, plus most of them have very modern and exciting designs.

Chapter 3: Bread Machine Techniques

The processes that occur in a bread machine are not that different than those you use when making bread by hand. They are just less work and mess. The primary techniques used in making bread from a bread machine are:

Mixing and resting.

The ingredients are mixed together well and then allowed to rest before kneading.

Kneading.

This technique creates long strands of gluten. Kneading squishes, stretches, turns, and presses the dough for 20 to 30 minutes, depending on the machine and setting.

First rise.

This is also called bulk fermentation. Yeast converts the sugar into alcohol, which provides flavor, and carbon dioxide, which provides structure as it inflates the gluten framework.

Stir down (1 and 2).

The paddles rotate to bring the loaf down and redistribute the dough before the second and third rise.

Second and third rise.

 The second rise is about 15 minutes. At the end of the third rise, the loaf will almost double in size.

Baking.

There will be one final growth spurt for the yeast in the dough in the first 5 minutes or so of the baking process, and the bread bakes into the finished loaf. Baking time and temperature will depend on the size, type, and crust setting of the loaf.

Cycles and Settings

Always remember to check the instructions on your bread machine. It varies across different models and types. So, before you start baking, make sure you know how to program your bread machine for the best quality bread. Your bread machine should come with a timing chart for the different types of bread.

There are bread machines that have their own weighing scale to ensure a proportionate amount of bread inside the machine. Check the capacity of your bread machine.

The idea of choosing a bread machine can be overwhelming, but most machines have a similar assortment of programmed cycles with precise times and temperatures, so different breads turn out perfectly—or close to perfect. While they may be called slightly different things the most common include:

Basic- This is the most commonly used settings. Often used for traditional white loaves. This setting is what will be used for a number of savory yeast recipes. This setting should not be used when making sweet breads which can cause over proofing and will result in overflowing.

Whole Wheat- If you are making a bread that uses whole wheat flour, then this is the setting you will use. Whole wheat flour requires a longer bake time. If you use a wheat gluten ingredient, then you may be able to use the basic setting instead. Double check your user manual to understand which settings is best based on the ingredients you are using.

Gluten Free- Many of the recipes in this book are gluten free, so you may find yourself using this setting more than the others. Most of the time the flours used in these recipes act differently than the everyday all-purpose flour or even wheat flour. Many gluten free recipes will vary slightly or significantly, but most ingredients should be set out and used at room temperature. Many of these breads, although gluten free, will still require a rise time.

Sweet Bread- This setting is also used often. This setting is what will be used for most sweet bread recipes that include yeast.

French- This setting is what will be used for not just French breads, but different types of artisan breads. When using this settings, you will have a bread that comes out with a crispy crust like that of a French or Italian loaf.

Quick/Rapid- This setting may also be labeled either quick cycle or rapid time. These breads will bake quickly and have short rise times. If using a rapid rising yeast, you can sometimes use this setting. To use this setting correctly, consult the user manual of your specific machine to ensure proper use.

Quick Bread- This setting is used for most breads that require no rising times and can be baked immediately. Banana bread is one example of a recipe you would use this setting for. This setting can also be used to bake cakes in your bread machine as well.

Jam- Some bread machine will offer special settings such as jam. This setting allows you to make your own homemade jams.

Dough- This is another specialty setting that some bread machine may offer. The dough setting can be used to make the dough for different breads, pies crust, and even cookie dough.

Other/Custom- This might include the option to extend baking or rise times by increments, preset baking times, or some other function that is explained in your manual.

Chapter 4: Tips For Bread

Storing Your Bread

Bread machine bread is so delicious, you might create more than you, your family, and your friends can eat in one sitting. Here are some tips for storing your bread machine creations:

Dough. After the kneading cycle, remove the dough from the machine. If you plan on using the dough within three days, you can store it in the refrigerator. Form the dough into a disk and place it in a sealable freezer bag, or store the dough in a lightly oiled bowl covered with plastic wrap. Yeast action will not stop in the refrigerator, so punch the dough down until it is completely chilled, and then once a day. When you are ready to bake bread, remove the dough from the refrigerator, shape it, let it rise, and bake. Bread machine dough has no preservatives, so freeze it if you aren't baking it in three days. Form the dough into a disk and place it in a sealable freezer bag. You can freeze bread dough for up to a month. When you are ready to bake the bread, remove the dough from the freezer, store it in the refrigerator overnight, shape it, let it rise, and bake. You can shape the dough into braids, loaves, knots, or other shapes before refrigerating or freezing it. Wrap the shapes tightly and store in the refrigerator (if you are baking within 24 hours) or the freezer. At the right time, unwrap the dough, allow it to rise at room temperature, and bake it.

Baked Bread. Once your baked bread is cooled, wrap the loaf in plastic wrap or a freezer bag and place it in the refrigerator or freezer. You can freeze baked bread for up to 6 months. To thaw the bread, remove it from the freezer, unwrap the loaf partially, and let it sit at room temperature. If you want to serve warm bread after refrigerating or freezing a loaf, wrap the bread in aluminum foil, and bake it in an oven preheated to 300°F for 10 to 15 minutes.

Storing the Leftover Bread

Top Storage Tips

Storing bread isn't always easy. If you manage not to eat all of the delicious goodies that you bake, you should find the best ways to store them so that you can keep them fresh longer. There are plenty of different things to keep in mind when it comes to storing bread, but homemade bread is especially delicate. Here are some tips to help you get the most out of your storage:

Don't store bread in the refrigerator. While this might seem like the freshness solution, it actually changes the alignment of the starch molecules, which is what causes bread to go stale. If you have leftovers from what you have baked, keep it on the counter or in the bread box.

Make sure that you don't leave bread sitting out for too long. Once you cut into a loaf, you have a limited amount of time to wrap it up and secure the freshness inside. If the interior is exposed to the air for too long, it will start to harden and go stale much quicker.

If your home or the bread itself is warm, do not put it in a plastic bag. The warmth will encourage condensation, which will prompt mold growth in the warm, moist environment. Wait until bread cools completely before storing it.

Pre-sliced and store-bought bread are going to go bad much quicker, simply because of all of the exposure and additives (which, ironically, are sometimes to retain freshness). If you're making your own bread with your bread machine, and you manage to have leftovers, these tips will make sure that you get the most out of your bread.

Moisture Matters

Just as with the baking process, the humidity and moisture in your home will affect the lifespan of your bread. It will also affect the storage options that you have. If the weather is more humid, you could leave bread on the counter overnight. However, it may have a softer crust as a result. Too much humidity means you need to store your bread in airtight containers and remove as much air and moisture as you can before storage.

That means letting the bread cool to room temperature before putting into plastic bags or containers. You will also want to hold off on slicing your bread when it first comes out of the bread machine. Unless you are going to eat the entire loaf within a short period of time, the best plan is to wait. When you cut into warm bread, steam comes out. That steam is moisture, which is helping the bread stay fresh and delicious. If you cut it too soon, you'll lose that freshness.

If you leave bread out on the counter and it is too dry, it will quickly turn into a brick. The lack of humidity is too much for fresh bread, and even too much for most store bought varieties. Moisture is a balance, and you have to find what works for your bread, and in your home. Remember that whole grain bread, French bread, and other harder bread will generally last much longer than soft sandwich bread.

If you store your bread in plastic too soon or for too long, the crust will go soft, as we mentioned before. However, you can avoid this by leaving the bread on the counter or wrapping it loosely with a cloth or paper once it is cool. For crust lovers, this is crucial. It's all about figuring out what works in your home and with your tastes, so feel free to experiment with storage solutions, too.

To Freeze or Not to Freeze?

You CAN freeze your bread. However, you simply have to be sure that you are doing it the right way. First of all, make sure that the bread is cooled to room temperature and that you have a paper or cloth wrapped around it to help collect and retain the moisture. Seal it tightly or wrap it securely, and store away for up to six months. Ideally use a vacuum sealer to make sure the bread is completely sealed.

The difficulty in freezing bread and other baked goods is not actually in the freezing process, but the thawing. It is critical that you take the bread out of the freezer ahead of time. Rather than defrosting it in the microwave or oven, you need to let it thaw completely. This will allow the bread to re-absorb any moisture that it lost during the freezing process, keeping it fresh and delicious. Once the bread comes to room temperature, you can toss it in the oven for a few minutes to warm it up.

Reheating bread is tricky. You will need to make sure that you give it the time that it needs to rest and prepare for the next step in the process. Moisture is the biggest problem with reheating or storing bread, and freezing can affect that in many different ways. It is going to be up to you to figure out the best ways to store and reheat your bread, but these tips should definitely help.

Other Storage Solutions

There is also the option of the bread box. Many bakers have been using these for centuries, and although they aren't as popular now as they were 20 years ago, they do still exist. Is a bread box the right choice for your bread? Consider a few things:

The type of material the box is made of. Metal versus wood boxes makes a big difference. It might also affect the storage and shelf-life based on other elements.

Is the box airtight? You'll need to decide whether or not this is something that you need, based on the humidity and standard temperature of your home. Most bread boxes are not sealed, but they still provide better bread storage than just leaving it on the counter, or losing the delicious crust by storing it in a plastic bag.

What type of bread are you storing? All breads are different and react differently when stored. Make sure that you take the time to get to know your bread varieties, as well as what is best for them.

Mistakes When Making Bread

Your success making bread in a bread machine can be affected by many different factors, which means a recipe that turns out a wonderful loaf one day may not produce the same loaf a week later. The bread will probably still be delicious, but it might not look exactly right. Here are some common bread-making issues:

No rise

- Yeast is old or stored improperly

- Measurement of ingredients is wrong

- Flour has low gluten content

- Too little yeast

- Temperature of ingredients is too high

- Temperature of ingredients is too low

- Too much salt

- Too much or too little sugar

Coarse texture

- Too much liquid

- Too little salt

- Too much yeast

- Fruit or vegetables too moist

- Weather too warm or humid

Crust too light

- Crust setting is too light

- Too little sugar

- Recipe size is too large for the bucket

Too much rise

- Too much yeast

- Too little salt

- Water temperature is incorrect

- Bucket is too small for the recipe size

Dense and short

- Bread doesn't rise (see No rise)

- Ingredients were added in the wrong order

- Dough is too dry; there is too much flour (not enough liquid)

- Size of the bucket is too large for the recipe

- Too much whole-grain flour or whole grains

- Too much dried fruit

- Too many other ingredients such as vegetables, nuts, or coconut

Crust too thick

- Bread is left in the machine after the baking cycle is complete

- Flour has too little gluten

- Bread doesn't rise high enough (see No rise)

Sunken top

- Bread machine was opened during baking cycle

- Humid or warm weather

- Too much liquid in the recipe

- Liquid ingredients are too warm

- Ingredients were measured wrong or out of proportion

- Bread rose too far, disrupting the baking and cooling cycles

- Too much yeast

Mushroom top

- Too much yeast

- Too much water

- Ingredients are out of proportion or measured wrong

- Too much sugar or too many sweet ingredients

- Size of the bucket is too small for the recipe

Gummy

- Too much sugar

- Too much liquid or too many wet ingredients

- Temperature outside the machine is too cold

- Thermostat in the machine is defective

Crust too dark

- Crust setting is too dark

- Bread is left in the machine after the baking cycle is complete

- Too much sugar

Pro Tips to Make Perfect Bread

Whether you're just baking bread for the first time or you just want to bake better goodies, this section will give you all kinds of helpful insight to ensure that you make the most of your baking. From important elements to quick fixes and even simple basics, you'll find it all here.

Measurements Make a Difference

When it comes to baking, measurements are not merely a suggestion. Rather, they are a science. You have to be very careful about measuring out your ingredients. For starters, make sure that you go to a kitchen store or shop online to supply your kitchen with actual measuring tools. Make sure that you have liquid and dry measuring tools in various sizes.

The biggest mistakes that you want to avoid include:

Don't use liquid measures for dry ingredients, And vice versa

Tablespoons and teaspoons are interchangeable for liquid and dry. Cups, however, are not. If you need two cups of water, it needs to be two liquid cups. Don't believe there's a difference? Use a dry cup measure and fill it with water. Then, pour it into your liquid measuring cup. You'll quickly see that the measurement is less than exact.

Don't skip the salt!

Unless you are specifically altering a recipe for sodium content (in which case you should find a low or no sodium version), salt is an ingredient for a reason and you cannot leave it out. Even if it seems like it wouldn't make a difference, it could ruin a recipe.

Get a conversion chart, app, or magnet for the fridge

There are plenty of kitchen conversion guides out there that you can keep on hand. That way, if you need to convert measurements or make substitutions, you know exactly how to do it. You'll find all of your cooking and baking to be more enjoyable when you have conversions and substitutions at hand at all times.

If you're still in the beginner stages, you'll want to stick to the book as best as you can until you get the hang of things. Once you branch out and start to experiment, you can toss these rules out the window (except the liquid/dry measure one). The deliciousness of baking is in the details, and you cannot afford to make simple mistakes when it comes to measurements. There is a reason for the recipe, so if you want to get the best result, follow the instructions to the letter.

Quality Matters

When you are baking anything, the quality of the ingredients that you use will make a difference. It isn't to say that the store brand flour isn't as good as the name brand because it very well might be. However, you should be careful in choosing higher quality ingredients in order to get better results. If you have the choice, go to a baker's supply or a local bakery outlet to buy the good stuff at better prices. If not, make sure that you get to know your basic ingredients and which ones are best.

The more familiar you get with your own baking abilities and preferences, the more you will be able to decide for yourself where quality matters most. Until then, keep these tips in mind. Also, remember that higher protein content counts with your flour if you're baking bread. More protein means stronger gluten, which makes better bread. Cake flour has a softer texture and lower protein count, which makes it ideal for baking cakes and other desserts.

Recipes All Have a Reason

A lot of people prefer just to "throw in" the ingredients or measure hastily, which is fine if you're an expert or you're baking something that you've made 100 times before. If, however, you are trying to replicate something out of a recipe book, you need to follow the recipe. Even a single missed ingredient or mismeasurement can turn your bread into something completely different than what you wanted.

It's not like you are going to ruin everything by taking on baking with reckless abandon. If you're new at the bread machine game, though, you should get used to what you're doing before you throw caution to the wind and throw the recipe aside once you remind yourself of the baking temperature.

Even if you concoct your own recipes over time, you'll want to write down at least a rough estimate of what the measurement is. It's hard to share recipes that don't have finite measurements. While you might know exactly how much a "little" salt is, other people can't measure that accurately. Cooking takes skill, but baking is a science, and it should be treated as such.

Stop: Check Your Settings

Again, the process is important. In that, you should also be sure that you check the settings of your bread machine before you start any new baking program. Even if you think you left it on the right setting or programmed the right feature, you need to double check every time. There is nothing worse than waiting an entire hour to realize that you've been using the wrong setting. At that point, your recipe will most likely be ruined.

For beginners, the pre-programmed settings should be perfect, for the most part. There are a lot more options for those who are more experienced with bread machines like the bread machine, and everyone will get there eventually. When in doubt, use the programs and features on the machine, and let it make the hard decisions for you. You'll get great results and if the program isn't exactly right, you'll at least have a starting point to begin making adjustments.

Buttermilk Basics

Some people might not even understand exactly what buttermilk is. You don't have to be embarrassed; a lot of people don't know what this weird baking ingredient is for. Buttermilk, traditionally, was what was left after the cream was churned into butter. Most of the buttermilk that you find on the shelves today is cultured or made.

Buttermilk is used because it adds a slight tang to baked goods. It also increases the rise of the bread or pastry by reacting with the baking soda in the recipe. Buttermilk is in a lot of bread and dessert recipes. However, not everyone just happens to keep buttermilk around. If you aren't in the habit of keeping it around, or if you decide to bake something at the last minute, there is a solution. You can take a liquid measuring cup (one cup is fine). In a measuring cup, add a tablespoon of lemon juice in the. Next, add milk up to half cup mark. Allow it to sit for a little bit, and voila, you have homemade buttermilk.

Try Something New

Experimenting is good. If you're a novice at baking bread or just starting to learn your bread machine, you might not want to stray too far from the traditional. However, if you are willing to make mistakes for the sake of success, experiment away! As you get more experienced in baking breads with your bread machine, you will be more comfortable in changing things up and seeing what all you can make on your own.

You can try ingredient substitutions, such as the common use of applesauce as a sweetener in baked goods. You can add ingredients to existing recipes, change baking times and temperatures, and even try and create your own great recipes using your bread machine. The sky is truly the limit, and even though this book includes 101 great recipes for you to try (see chapter seven), you are still going to find plenty of other great ways to enjoy baking with your bread machine.

Consistency Checks

The big difference with baking bread, compared to other cooking, is that you need to keep an eye on the consistency. While the good old "lightly brown" rule does stand in most cases, the consistency can be very different in a bread machine like the bread machine. Make sure that you capitalize on that "pause" feature and give yourself the chance to check in on your baked goods from time to time to ensure that they turn out their best.

You don't need to interrupt your baking processes too often. Once should be enough. When you're making bread, it's a great idea to pause to remove the paddle, and at the same time, check on the bread and see how it's coming along. Not only does that allow you to ensure that the consistency is right, but it also allows you to get that paddle out before it's baked into the loaf and becomes a chore to remove.

Chapter 5: Keto Bread Recipes

Garlic, herb and cheese bread

Prep time: 5 minutes

Serves: 12

Difficulty: Intermediate

Ingredients:

- ½ cup ghee
- 6 eggs
- 2 cups almond flour
- 1 tsp baking powder
- ½ tsp xanthan gum
- 1 cup cheddar cheese, shredded
- 1 tbsp garlic powder
- 1 tbsp parsley
- ½ tbsp. oregano
- ½ tsp salt

Directions:

1. Lightly beat eggs and ghee before pouring into bread machine pan.
2. Add the remaining ingredients to the pan.

3. Set bread machine to gluten free.

4. When the bread is done, remove bread machine pan from the bread machine.

5. Let cool slightly before transferring to a cooling rack.

6. You can store your bread for up to 5 days in the refrigerator.

Nutritional Value Per Serving:

Calories 156

Carbohydrates 4 g

Fats 13 g

Sugar 4g

Protein 5 g

Pumpkin and sunflower seed bread

Prep time: 8 minutes

Serves: 10

Difficulty: expert

Ingredients:

- ½ cup ground psyllium husk
- ½ cup chia seeds
- ½ cup pumpkin seeds
- ½ cup sunflower seeds
- 2 tbsp ground flaxseed
- 1 tsp baking soda
- ¼ tsp salt
- 3 tbsp coconut oil, melted
- 1 ¼ cup egg whites
- ½ cup almond milk

Directions:

1. Place all wet ingredients into bread machine pan first.
2. Add dry ingredients.
3. Set bread machine to the gluten free setting.

4. When the bread is done, remove bread machine pan from the bread machine.

5. Let cool slightly before transferring to a cooling rack.

6. You can store your bread for up to 5 days in the refrigerator.

Nutritional Value Per Serving:

Calories 155

Carbohydrates 4 g

Fats 8 g

Sugar 3g

Protein 5 g

Rosemary bread

Prep time: 4 minutes

Serves: 12

Difficulty: intermediate

Ingredients:

- 2 ½ cups almond flour
- ¼ cup coconut flour
- ½ cup ghee
- 8 oz cream cheese
- 5 eggs
- 1 tsp rosemary
- 1 tsp sage, ground
- 2 tsp parsley
- 1 tsp baking powder

Directions:

1. Slightly beat eggs and ghee together in a bowl then pour into bread machine pan.

2. Add all the remaining ingredients.

3. Set bread machine to the French bread setting

4. When the bread is done, remove bread machine pan from the bread machine.

5. Let cool slightly before transferring to a cooling rack.

6. You can store your bread for up to 7 days in the refrigerator

Nutritional Value Per Serving:

Calories 140

Carbohydrates 2.8 g

Fats 14 g

Protein 5 g

Savory herb blend bread

Prep time: 7 minutes

Serves: 16

Difficulty: intermediate

Ingredients:

- 1 cup almond flour
- ½ cup coconut flour
- 1 cup parmesan cheese
- ¾ tsp baking powder
- 3 eggs
- 3 tbsp coconut oil
- ½ tbsp rosemary
- ½ tsp thyme, ground
- ½ tsp sage, ground
- ½ tsp oregano
- ½ tsp garlic powder
- ½ tsp onion powder
- ¼ tsp salt
-

Directions:

1. Light beat eggs and coconut oil together before adding to bread machine pan.

2. Add all the remaining ingredients to bread machine pan.

3. Set bread machine to the gluten free setting.

4. When the bread is done, remove bread machine pan from the bread machine.

5. Let cool slightly before transferring to a cooling rack.

6. You can store your bread for up to 7 days .

Nutritional Value Per Serving:

Calories 170

Carbohydrates 6 g

Fats 15 g

Protein 9 g

Cinnamon almond bread

Prep time: 3 minutes

Serves: 10

Difficulty: expert

Ingredients:

- 2 tbsps. coconut flour
- 1 tsp baking soda
- 2 cups almond flour
- 2 tbsps. coconut oil
- ¼ cup flaxseed, ground
- 1 egg white
- 1 ½ tsp lemon juice
- 5 eggs
- 2 tbsps. erythritol
- ½ tsp salt
- 1 tbsp. cinnamon

Directions:

1. Pour wet ingredients into bread machine pan.
2. Add dry ingredients to the bread machine pan.
3. Set bread machine to the gluten free setting.

4. When the bread is done, remove bread machine pan from the bread machine.

5. Let cool slightly before transferring to a cooling rack.

6. You can store your bread for up to 5 days.

Nutritional Value Per Serving:

Calories 220

Carbohydrates 10 g

Fats 15 g

Protein 9 g

Cheesy Garlic Bread

Prep time: 30 minutes

Serves: 10

Difficulty: expert

Ingredients:

- ¾ cup mozzarella, shredded
- ½ cup almond flour
- 2 tbsps. cream cheese
- 1 tbsp. garlic, crushed
- 1 tbsp. parsley
- 1 tsp baking powder
- Salt, to taste
- 1 egg

For the toppings:

- 2 tbsps. melted butter
- ½ tsp parsley
- 1 tsp garlic clove, minced

Directions:

1. Mix together your topping ingredients and set aside.

2. Pour the remaining wet ingredients into the bread machine pan.

3. Add the dry ingredients.

4. Set bread machine to the gluten free setting.

5. When the bread is done, remove bread machine pan from the bread machine.

6. Let cool slightly before transferring to a cooling rack.

7. Once on a cooling rack, drizzle with the topping mix.

8. You can store your bread for up to 7 days.

Nutritional Value Per Serving:

Calories: 29

Carbohydrates: 1g

Protein: 2g

Fiber 1g

Fat: 2g

Almond flour bread

Prep time: 4 minutes

Serves: 10

Difficulty: intermediate

Ingredients:

- 4 egg whites
- 2 egg yolks
- 2 cups almond flour
- ¼ cup butter, melted
- 2 tbsp psyllium husk powder
- 1 ½ tsp baking powder
- ½ tsp xanthan gum
- Salt
- ½ cup + 2 tbsps. warm water
- 2 ¼ tsp yeast

Directions:

1. Use a small mixing bowl to combine all dry ingredients, except for the yeast.

2. In the bread machine pan add all wet ingredients.

3. Add all of your dry ingredients, from the small mixing bowl, in the bread machine pan. Top with the yeast.

4. Set the bread machine to the basic bread setting.

5. When the bread is done, remove bread machine pan from the bread machine.

6. Let cool slightly before transferring to a cooling rack.

7. The bread can be stored for up to 4 days on the counter and for up to 3 months in the freezer.

Nutritional Value Per Serving:

Calories 110

Carbohydrates 2.4 g

Fats 10 g

Protein 4 g

Coconut flour bread

Prep time: 5 minutes

Serves: 12

Difficulty: intermediate

Ingredients:

- 6 eggs

- ½ cup coconut flour

- 2 tbsp psyllium husk

- ¼ cup olive oil

- 1 ½ tsp salt

- 1 tsp xanthan gum

- 1 teaspon baking powder

- 2 ¼ tsp yeast

Directions:

1. Use a small mixing bowl to combine all dry ingredients, except for the yeast.

2. In the bread machine pan add all wet ingredients.

3. Add all of your dry ingredients, from the small mixing bowl, in the bread machine pan. Top with the yeast.

4. Set the bread machine to the basic bread setting.

5. When the bread is done, remove bread machine pan from the bread machine.

6. Let cool slightly before transferring to a cooling rack.

7. The bread can be stored for up to 4 days on the counter and for up to 3 months in the freezer.

Nutritional Value Per Serving:

Calories 174

Carbohydrates 4 g

Fats 15 g

Protein 7 g

Cloud bread loaf

Prep time: 5 minutes

Serves: 10

Difficulty: intermediate

Ingredients:

- 6 egg whites
- 6 egg yolks
- ½ cup whey protein powder, unflavored
- ½ tsp cream of tartar
- 6 oz sour cream
- ½ tsp baking powder
- ¼ tsp garlic powder
- ¼ tsp onion powder
- ¼ tsp salt

Directions:

1. Using a hand mixer beat egg whites and cream of tartar together until you have stiff peaks forming. Set aside.

2. Combine all other ingredients into another bowl and mix together.

3. Fold the mixtures together, a little at a time.

4. Pour mixture into your bread machine pan.

5. Set the bread machine to quick bread.

6. When the bread is done, remove bread machine pan from the bread machine.

7. Let cool slightly before transferring to a cooling rack.

8. The bread can be stored for up to 3 days on the counter.

Nutritional Value Per Serving:

Calories 90

Carbohydrates 2 g

Fats 7 g

Protein 6 g

Sourdough bread

Prep time: 6 minutes

Serves: 10

Difficulty: expert

Ingredients:

- ½ cup almond flour

- ½ cup coconut flour

- ½ cup ground flaxseed

- 1/3 cup psyllium husk powder

- 1 tsp baking soda

- 1 tsp Himalayan salt

- 2 eggs

- 6 egg whites

- ¾ cup buttermilk

- ¼ cup apple cider vinegar

- ½ cup warm water

Directions:

1. Combine the flours, flaxseed, psyllium husk, baking soda, and salt into a bowl, mix together, and set aside.

2. Place eggs, egg whites, and buttermilk into bread machine baking pan.

3. Add dry ingredients on top, then pour over vinegar and warm water.

4. Set bread machine to French setting (or a similar longer setting).

5. Check dough during kneading process to see if more water may be needed.

6. When the bread is done, remove bread machine pan from the bread machine.

7. Let cool slightly before transferring to a cooling rack.

8. The bread can be stored for up to 10 days in the fridge or for 3 months in the freezer.

Nutritional Value Per Serving:

Calories 85

Carbohydrates 4 g

Fats 4 g

Protein 6 g

Seeded loaf

Prep time: 5 minutes

Serves: 16

Difficulty: intermediate

Ingredients:

- 7 eggs
- 1 cup almond flour
- ½ cup butter
- 2 tbsp olive oil
- 2 tbsp chia seeds
- 2 tbsp sesame seeds
- 1 tsp baking soda
- ½ tsp xanthan gum
- ¼ tsp salt

Directions:

1. Add eggs and butter to the bread machine pan.
2. Top with all other ingredients.
3. Set bread machine to the gluten free setting.
4. Once done remove from bread machine and transfer to a cooling rack.

5. This bread can be stored in the fridge for up to 5 days or 3 weeks in the freezer.

Nutritional Value Per Serving:

Calories 190

Carbohydrates 8 g

Fats 18 g

Protein 18 g

Simple keto bread

Prep time: 3 minutes

Serves: 8

Difficulty: intermediate

Ingredients:

- 3 cups almond flour
- 2 tbsp inulin
- 1 tbsp whole milk
- ½ tsp salt
- 2 tsp active yeast
- 1 ¼ cups warm water
- 1 tbsp olive oil

Directions:

1. Use a small mixing bowl to combine all dry ingredients, except for the yeast.
2. In the bread machine pan add all wet ingredients.
3. Add all of your dry ingredients, from the small mixing bowl, in the bread machine pan. Top with the yeast.
4. Set the bread machine to the basic bread setting.
5. When the bread is done, remove bread machine pan from the bread machine.

6. Let cool slightly before transferring to a cooling rack.

7. The bread can be stored for up to 5 days on the counter and for up to 3 months in the freezer.

Nutritional Value Per Serving:

Calories 85

Carbohydrates 4 g

Fats 7 g

Protein 3 g

Classic keto bread

Prep time: 3 minutes

Serves: 10

Difficulty: intermediate

Ingredients:

- 7 eggs
- ½ cup ghee
- 2 cups almond flour
- 1 tbsp baking powder
- ¼ tsp salt

Directions:

1. Pour eggs and ghee into bread machine pan.
2. Add remaining ingredients.
3. Set bread machine to quick setting.
4. Allow bread machine to complete its cycle.
5. When the bread is done, remove bread machine pan from the bread machine.
6. Let cool slightly before transferring to a cooling rack.
7. The bread can be stored for up to 4 days on the counter and for up to 3 months in the freezer.

Nutritional Value Per Serving:

Calories 167

Carbohydrates 2 g

Fats 16 g

Protein 5 g

Collagen keto bread

Prep time: 5 minutes

Serves: 12

Difficulty: expert

Ingredients:

- ½ cup collagen protein, unflavored grass-fed

- 6 tbsp almond flour

- 5 eggs

- 1 tbsp coconut oil, melted

- 1 tsp baking powder

- 1 tsp xanthan gum

- ¼ tsp Himalayan pink salt

Directions:

1. Pour all wet ingredients into bread machine bread pan.

2. Add dry ingredients to the bread machine pan.

3. Set bread machine to the gluten free setting

4. When the bread is done, remove bread machine pan from the bread machine.

5. Let cool slightly before transferring to a cooling rack.

6. The bread can be stored for up to 4 days on the counter and for up to 3 months in the freezer.

Nutritional Value Per Serving:

Calories 77

Carbohydrates 6 g

Fats 14 g

Protein 5 g

Banana cake loaf

Prep time: 4 minutes

Serves: 12

Difficulty: Beginner

Ingredients:

- 1 ½ cups almond flour
- 1 tsp baking powder
- ½ cup butter
- 1 ½ cups erythritol
- 2 eggs
- 2 bananas, extra ripe, mashed
- 2 tsp whole milk

Directions:

1. Mix butter, eggs, and milk together in a mixing bowl.
2. Mash bananas with a fork and add in the mashed bananas.
3. Mix all dry ingredients together in a separate small bowl.
4. Slowly combine dry ingredients with wet ingredients.
5. Pour mixture into bread machine pan.
6. Set bread machine for bake.

7. When the cake is done remove from bread machine and transfer to a cooling rack.

8. Allow to cool completely before serving.

9. You can store your banana cake loaf bread for up to 5 days in the refrigerator.

Nutritional Value Per Serving:

Calories 175

Carbohydrates 6 g

Fats 14 g

Protein 5 g

Almond butter brownies

Prep time: 3 minutes

Serves: 14

Difficulty: intermediate

Ingredients:

- 1 cup almond butter

- 2 tbsp cocoa powder, unsweetened

- ½ cup erythritol

- 1 egg

- 3 tbsp almond milk, unsweetened

Directions:

1. Beat egg and almond butter together in a mixing bowl.

2. Add in erythritol and cocoa powder.

3. If the mixture is too crumbly or dry, add in almond milk until you have a smooth consistency.

4. Pour mixture into bread machine pan.

5. Set bread machine to bake.

6. When done remove from bread machine and transfer to a cooling rack.

7. Cool completely before serving, You can store for up to 5 days in the refrigerator.

Nutritional Value Per Serving:

Calories 141

Carbohydrates 3 g

Fats 12 g

Protein 5 g

Almond butter bread

Prep time: 3 minutes

Serves: 8

Difficulty: intermediate

Ingredients:

- 1 cup coconut almond butter, creamy
- 3 eggs
- ½ tsp baking soda
- 1 tbsp apple cider vinegar

Directions:

1. Combine all ingredients in a food processor.
2. When the mixture is smooth transfer to bread machine baking pan.
3. Set bread machine to bake.
4. When done baking, remove from the pan from your bread machine.
5. Allow to cool completely before slicing.
6. You can store for up to 5 days in the refrigerator.

Nutritional Value Per Serving:

Calories 175

Carbohydrates 6 g

Fats 14 g

Protein 5 g

Cinnamon cake

Prep time: 7 minutes

Serves: 12

Difficulty: intermediate

Ingredients:

- ½ cup erythritol
- ½ cup butter
- ½ tbsp vanilla extract
- 1 ¾ cups almond flour
- 1 ½ tsp baking powder
- 1 ½ tsp cinnamon
- ¼ tsp sea salt
- 1 ½ cup carrots, grated
- 1 cup pecans, chopped

Directions:

1. Grate carrots and place in a food processor.
2. Add in the rest of the ingredients, except the pecans, and process until well- incorporated.
3. Fold in pecans.
4. Pour mixture into bread machine pan.

5. Set bread machine to bake.

6. When baking is complete remove from bread machine and transfer to a cooling rack.

7. Allow to cool completely before slicing. (You can also top with a sugar-free cream cheese frosting, see recipe below).

8. You can store for up to 5 days in the refrigerator.

Nutritional Value Per Serving:

Calories 350

Carbohydrates 8 g

Fats 34 g

Protein 7 g

Classic gluten free bread

Prep time: 5 minutes

Serves: 12

Difficulty: intermediate

Ingredients:

- ½ cup butter, melted
- 3 tbsp coconut oil, melted
- 6 eggs
- 2/3 cup sesame seed flour
- 1/3 cup coconut flour
- 2 tsp baking powder
- 1 tsp psyllium husks
- ½ tsp xanthan gum
- ½ tsp salt

Directions:

1. Pour in eggs, melted butter, and melted coconut oil into your bread machine pan.

2. Add the remaining ingredients to the bread machine pan.

3. Set bread machine to gluten free.

4. When the bread is done, remove bread machine pan from the bread machine.

5. Let cool slightly before transferring to a cooling rack.

6. You can store your bread for up to 3 days.

Nutritional Value Per Serving:

Calories 146

Carbohydrates 1.2 g

Fats 14 g

Protein 3.5 g

Gluten free chocolate zucchini bread

Prep time: 5 minutes

Serves: 12

Difficulty: expert

Ingredients:

- 1 ½ cups coconut flour
- ¼ cup unsweetened cocoa powder
- ½ cup erythritol
- ½ tsp cinnamon
- 1 tsp baking soda
- 1 tsp baking powder
- ¼ tsp salt
- ¼ cup coconut oil, melted
- 4 eggs
- 1 tsp vanilla
- 2 cups zucchini, shredded

Directions:

1. Shred the zucchini and use paper towels to drain excess water, set aside.

2. Lightly beat eggs with coconut oil then add to bread machine pan.

3. Add the remaining ingredients to the pan.

4. Set bread machine to gluten free.

5. When the bread is done, remove bread machine pan from the bread machine.

6. Let cool slightly before transferring to a cooling rack.

7. You can store your bread for up to 5 days.

Nutritional Value Per Serving:

Calories 185

Carbohydrates 6 g

Fats 17 g

Protein 5 g

Not your everyday bread

Prep time: 7 minutes

Serves: 12

Difficulty: intermediate

Ingredients:

- 2 tsp active dry yeast
- 2 tbsp inulin
- ½ cup warm water
- ¾ cup almond flour
- ¼ cup golden flaxseed, ground
- 2 tbsp whey protein isolate
- 2 tbsp psyllium husk finely ground
- 2 tsp xanthan gum
- 2 tsp baking powder
- 1 tsp salt
- ¼ tsp cream of tartar
- ¼ tsp ginger, ground
- 1 egg
- 3 egg whites
- 2 tbsp ghee

- 1 tbsp apple cider vinegar

- ¼ cup sour cream

Directions:

1. Pour wet ingredients into bread machine pan.

2. Add dry ingredients, with the yeast on top.

3. Set bread machine to basic bread setting.

4. When the bread is done, remove bread machine pan from the bread machine.

5. Let cool slightly before transferring to a cooling rack.

6. You can store your bread for up to 5 days.

Nutritional Value Per Serving:

Calories 175

Carbohydrates 6 g

Fats 14 g

Protein 5 g

Pumpkin bread

Prep time: 5 minutes

Serves: 8

Difficulty: intermediate

Ingredients:

- 6 eggs
- 8 tbsp butter, melted
- 2 cups almond flour
- 2 teaspoons baking powder
- ¼ teaspoon ground allspice
- ¼ teaspoon ground cloves
- ¼ teaspoon ground nutmeg
- ½ cup erythritol
- ½ cup pumpkin puree
- 1 tsp cinnamon
- 3 tbsps. sour cream
- 1 teaspoon vanilla
- 2 tbsp heavy cream

Directions:

1. In the bread machine pan add all the wet ingredients.

2. Then add the dry ingredients on top.

3. Set the bread machine to the gluten free bread setting.

4. When the bread is done, remove bread machine pan from the bread machine.

5. Let cool slightly before transferring to a cooling rack.

6. The bread can be stored for up to 5 days on the counter.

Nutritional Value Per Serving:

Calories 220

Carbohydrates 14 g

Fats 21 g

Protein 6 g

Zucchini bread with walnuts

Prep time: 4 minutes

Serves: 12

Difficulty: expert

Ingredients:

- 2 ½ cups almond flour

- ½ cup olive oil

- 1.5 cups erythritol

- 1 tsp vanilla extract

- ½ tsp nutmeg

- 3 large eggs

- 1 ½ tsp baking powder

- 1 cup grated zucchinis

- 1 tsp cinnamon

- ¼ tsp ginger

- ½ tsp salt

- ½ cup walnuts, chopped

Directions:

1. Grate zucchini and use a cheesecloth to squeeze excess water out and set aside.

2. Mix eggs, vanilla extract, and oil in bread machine pan.

3. Add almond flour, ginger, erythritol, salt, nutmeg, baking powder and cinnamon.

4. Add the zucchini to the bread machine pan and top with walnuts.

5. Set bread machine to gluten free.

6. When the bread is done, remove bread machine pan from the bread machine.

7. Let cool slightly before transferring to a cooling rack.

8. The bread can be stored for up to 5 days on the counter and for up to 3 months in the freezer.

Nutritional Value Per Serving:

Calories 160

Carbohydrates 3 g

Fats 16 g

Protein 4 g

Greek Olive Bread

Prep time: 15 minutes

Serves: 20

Difficulty: intermediate

Ingredients:

- 4 eggs

- 5 tbsps. ground flaxseed

- 2 tsp psyllium powder

- 2 tbsps. apple cider vinegar

- 1 tsp baking soda

- 1 tsp salt

- ½ cup sour cream

- ½ cup olive oil

- 1.8 oz black olives, chopped

- 1 tsp ground rosemary

- 1 ½ cups almond flour

- 1 tsp dried basil

Directions:

1. Beat eggs in a mixing bowl for about 5 minutes. Add olive oil slowly while you continue to beat the eggs. Add in sour

cream and apple cider vinegar and continue to beat for another 5 minutes.

2. Mix all of the remaining ingredients together in a separate smaller bowl.

3. Place all wet ingredients into bread machine pan.

4. Add the remaining ingredients to the bread pan.

5. Set bread machine to the French setting.

6. When the bread is done, remove bread machine pan from the bread machine.

7. Let cool slightly before transferring to a cooling rack.

8. The bread can be stored for up to 7 days on the counter.

Nutritional Value Per Serving:

Calories: 150

Carbohydrates: 3g

Protein: 3g

Fat: 14g

Veggie Loaf

Prep time: 20 minutes

Serves: 20

Difficulty: intermediate

Ingredients:

- 1/3 cup coconut flour
- 2 tablespoons chia Seed
- 2 tbsps. psyllium husk powder
- ¼ cup sunflower seeds
- ¼ cup pumpkin seeds
- 2 tbsp flax seed
- 1 cup almond flour
- 1 cup zucchini, grated
- 4 eggs
- ¼ cup coconut oil, melted
- 1 tbsp paprika
- 2 tsp cumin
- 2 tsp baking powder
- 2 tsp salt

Directions:

1. Grate carrots and zucchini, use a cheesecloth to drain excess water, set aside.

2. Mix eggs and coconut oil into bread machine pan.

3. Add the remaining ingredients to bread pan.

4. Set bread machine to quick bread setting.

5. When the bread is done, remove bread machine pan from the bread machine.

6. Let cool slightly before transferring to a cooling rack.

7. You can store your veggie loaf bread for up to 5 days in the refrigerator, or you can also be sliced and stored in the freezer for up to 3 months.

Nutritional Value Per Serving:

Calories: 150

Carbohydrates: 3g

Protein: 3g

Fat: 14g

Cajun Veggie Loaf

Prep time: 15 minutes

Serves: 12

Difficulty: expert

Ingredients:

- ½ cup water

- ¼ cup onion, chopped

- ½ cup green bell pepper, chopped

- 2 tsp garlic, chopped finely

- 2 tsp ghee

- 2 cups almond flour

- 1 tbsp inulin

- 1 tsp Cajun seasoning

- 1 tsp active dry yeast

Directions:

1. Add water and ghee to bread machine pan.

2. Add in the remaining ingredients.

3. Set bread machine to basic setting.

4. When done, remove from bread machine and allow to cool before slicing.

5. Let cool slightly before transferring to a cooling rack.

6. You can store your bread for up to 5 days in the refrigerator.

Nutritional Value Per Serving:

Calories: 101

Carbohydrates: 6g

Protein: 4g

Fat: 8g

Parmesan Italian Bread

Prep time: 16 minutes

Serves: 10

Difficulty: intermediate

Ingredients:

- 1 1/3 cup warm water

- 2 tbsps. olive oil

- 2 cloves of garlic, crushed

- 1 tbsp. basil

- 1 tbsp. oregano

- 1 tbsp. parsley

- 2 cups almond flour

- 1 tbsp. inulin

- ½ cup parmesan cheese, grated

- 1 tsp active dry yeast

Directions:

1. Pour all wet ingredients into bread machine pan.

2. Add all dry ingredients to pan.

3. Set bread machine to French bread.

4. When the bread is done, remove bread machine pan from the bread machine.

5. Let cool slightly before transferring to a cooling rack.

6. You can store your bread for up to 7 days.

Nutritional Value Per Serving:

Calories: 150

Carbohydrates: 14g

Protein: 5g

Fat: 5g

Bacon Jalapeño Cheesy Bread

Prep time: 22 minutes

Serves: 12

Difficulty: expert

Ingredients:

- 1 cup golden flaxseed, ground

- ¾ cup coconut flour

- 2 tsp baking powder

- ¼ tsp black pepper

- 1 tbsp. erythritol

- 1/3 cup pickled jalapeno

- 8 oz. cream cheese, full fat

- 4 eggs

- 3 cups sharp cheddar cheese, shredded + ¼ cup extra for the topping

- 3 tbsps. parmesan cheese, grated

- 1 ¼ cup almond milk

- 5 Bacon Slices (cooked and crumbled)

- ¼ cup rendered bacon grease (from frying the bacon)

Directions:

1. Cook the bacon in a larger frying pan, set aside to cool on paper towels. Save ¼ cup of bacon fat for the recipe, allow to cool slightly before using.

2. Add wet ingredients to bread machine pan, including the cooled bacon grease.

3. Add in the remaining ingredients.

4. Set the bread machine to the quick bread setting.

5. When the bread is done, remove bread machine pan from the bread machine.

6. Let cool slightly before transferring to a cooling rack.

7. Once on a cooling rack, top with the remaining cheddar cheese.

8. You can store your bread for up to 7 days.

Nutritional Value Per Serving:

Calories: 235

Carbohydrates: 5g

Protein: 11g

Fat: 17g

Raspberry Bread

Prep time: 20 minutes

Serves: 10

Difficulty: intermediate

Ingredients:

- 2 cups almond flour
- ½ cup coconut flour
- ½ cup ghee
- ½ cup coconut oil, melted
- ½ cup erythritol
- 4 eggs
- 1 tsp lemon juice
- ½ cup raspberries
- 2 tsp baking powder

Directions:

1. Lightly beat eggs before pouring into bread machine pan.
2. Add in melted coconut oil, ghee, and lemon juice to pan.
3. Add the remaining ingredients.
4. Set bread machine to quick bread.

5. When the bread is done, remove bread machine pan from the bread machine.

6. Let cool slightly before transferring to a cooling rack.

7. You can store your bread for up to 5 days.

Nutritional Value Per Serving:

Calories: 300

Carbohydrates: 14g

Protein: 5g

Fat: 30g

Whole-Wheat Sourdough Bread

Prep time: 10 minutes

Servings: 8

Difficulty: intermediate

Ingredients:

- ⅔ cups hot water

- ⅔ cup No-Yeast Whole-Wheat Sourdough Starter, fed, active, and at room temperature

- 4 teaspoons butter, melted

- 2 teaspoons sugar

- 1 teaspoon salt

- 1¼ teaspoons instant yeast

- 2 cups whole- almond flour

Directions:

1. Put all ingredients in the bread machine.

2. Set the machine to Whole-Wheat/Whole-Grain bread, select light or medium crust, and press Start.

3. When ready, remove the bread and allow about 5 minutes to cool the loaf.

4. Put it on a rack to cool it completely

Nutritional Value Per Serving:

Calories: 155

Fat: 2g

Carbohydrates: 2.9g

Fiber: 1g

Protein: 4g

Blueberry Muffin Bread

Prep time: 15 minutes

Serves: 12

Difficulty: beginner

Ingredients:

- ½ cup almond butter

- 1/3 cup coconut oil

- ½ cup almond flour

- ½ cup erythritol

- ½ tsp salt

- 2 tsp baking powder

- ½ cup almond milk, unsweetened

- 5 eggs

- ½ cup blueberries

Directions:

1. In a small microwaveable bowl, combine your almond butter and coconut oil. Heat for about 10 seconds to melt (it may need an extra 5 or more seconds to melt depending on your microwave).

2. Add the eggs into the bowl with the melted butter and oil and beat slightly.

3. Add the egg mixture into your bread machine pan.

104

4. Add the milk.

5. Use a separate small mixing bowl to combine all of your dry ingredients.

6. Pour dry ingredients on top of the wet mixture in your bread machine pan.

7. Set the bread machine to its basic bread setting.

8. Check the dough halfway through its kneading process to ensure it is smooth and tacky. If needed add a tablespoon more of flour if too wet, or a tablespoon of water if too dry.

9. Let the dough continue to knead and bake in the bread machine.

10. When the bread is done, remove bread machine pan from the bread machine.

11. Let cool slightly before transferring to a cooling rack.

12. You can store your bread for up to 4 days.

Nutritional Value Per Serving:

Calories: 156

Carbohydrates: 4g

Protein: 5g

Fat: 13g

Lemon Blueberry Bread

Prep time: 10 minutes

Serves: 10

Difficulty: intermediate

Ingredients:

- 2 cups almond flour

- ½ cup coconut flour

- ½ cup ghee

- ½ cup coconut oil, melted

- ½ cup erythritol

- 4 eggs

- 2 tbsps. lemon zest, about half a lemon

- 1 tsp lemon juice

- ½ cup blueberries

- 2 tsp baking powder

Directions:

1. Lightly beat eggs before pouring into your bread machine pan.

2. Add in melted coconut oil, ghee, and lemon juice to pan.

3. Add the remaining dry ingredients including blueberries and lemon zest to the bread machine pan.

4. Set bread machine to quick bread setting.

5. When the bread is done, remove bread machine pan from the bread machine.

6. Let cool slightly before transferring to a cooling rack.

7. You can store your bread for up to 5 days.

Nutritional Value Per Serving:

Calories: 300

Carbohydrates: 14g

Protein: 5g

Fat: 30g

Cheese Blend Bread

Prep time: 25 minutes

Serves: 12

Difficulty: intermediate

Ingredients:

- 5 oz. cream cheese
- ¼ cup ghee
- 2/3 cup almond flour
- ¼ cup coconut flour
- 3 tbsps. whey protein, unflavored
- 2 tsp baking powder
- ½ tsp Himalayan salt
- ½ cup parmesan cheese, shredded
- 3 tbsps. water
- 3 eggs
- ½ cup mozzarella cheese, shredded

Directions:

1. Place wet ingredients into bread machine pan.
2. Add dry ingredients.
3. Set the bread machine to the gluten free setting.

4. When the bread is done, remove bread machine pan from the bread machine.

5. Let cool slightly before transferring to a cooling rack.

6. You can store your bread for up to 5 days.

Nutritional Value Per Serving:

Calories: 132

Carbohydrates: 4g

Protein: 6g

Fat: 8 g

Strawberries And Cream Bread

Prep time: 18 minutes

Serves: 10

Difficulty: expert

Ingredients:

- ¾ cup whole milk

- ½ cup cream cheese

- ½ cup strawberries, sliced

- 1 tbsp. coconut oil, melted

- 1 tsp salt

- 2 tbsps. inulin

- 1 tbsp. chia seeds

- 3 cups almond Flour

- 2 tsp instant yeast

Directions:

1. Pour all wet ingredients into bread machine pan.

2. Add dry ingredients to pan.

3. Set bread machine to the sweet bread setting.

4. Check the dough during the kneading process to ensure more water does not need to be added. Otherwise just allow the bread machine to run its course.

5. When the bread is done, remove bread machine pan from the bread machine.

6. Let cool slightly before transferring to a cooling rack.

7. You can store your bread for up to 5 days.

Nutritional Value Per Serving:

Calories: 120

Carbohydrates: 5g

Protein: 4g

Fat: 10g

No-Yeast Sourdough Starter

Prep time: 10 minutes

Serves: 4 cups (64 servings)

Difficulty: expert

Ingredients:

- 2 cups all-purpose flour

- 2 cups chlorine-free bottled water, at room temperature

Directions:

1. Stir together the flour and water in a large glass bowl with a wooden spoon.

2. Loosely cover the bowl with plastic wrap and place it in a warm area for 3 to 4 days, stirring at least twice a day, or until bubbly.

3. Store the starter in the refrigerator in a covered glass jar, and stir it before using.

4. Replenish your starter by adding back the same amount you removed, in equal parts flour and water.

Nutritional Value Per Serving:

Calories: 14

Fat: 0g

Carbohydrates: 3g

Fiber: 0g

Protein: 0g

Bread with Walnuts and Garlic

Prep time: 4 hours

Servings: 10

Difficulty: expert

Ingredients:

- 3 cups almond flour
- 2 teaspoons dry yeast
- 1 cup walnuts
- 10 garlic cloves, chopped
- 10 tablespoons Olive oil
- 1 cup garlic butter, melted
- 2 cups water
- 2 teaspoons sugar
- 2 egg yolks
- Sea salt to taste

Directions:

1. Preheat the oven to 290°-320°Fahrenheit and roast the walnuts in the oven for 10-15 minutes until lightly browned and crispy. Set aside to cool completely. Grind the walnuts using a food processor.

2. Melt the unsalted butter by making it softer, by taking it out of the fridge and leaving for around 30 minutes or melt the butter using a frying pan. Meanwhile chop the garlic cloves.

3. Put the almond flour into the bowl and then add in the yeast, sugar, garlic, egg yolks, Olive oil and sea salt and mix until there is a smooth consistency and homogenous mass. Add in the walnuts.

4. Spoon the mixture into the bread machine and add in the water and melted softened garlic butter, mix well.

5. Lubricate the surface of the dough with the water or the egg yolk.

6. Now close the lid and turn the bread machine on the basic/white bread program.

7. After the breakfast wheat bread with garlic is ready, take it out and leave for 1 hour covered with the towel and then you can consume the bread, although we recommend eating your bread after 24 hours.

Nutritional Value Per Serving:

Calories: 100

Fat: 4g

Carbohydrates 4.6

Sugar 0g

Proteins: 2

Cheddar Herb Bread

Prep time

Serves: 16

Difficulty: expert

Ingredients:

- ½ cup butter, room temperature
- 6 eggs
- 1 tsp baking powder
- 2 cups almond flour
- ½ tsp xanthan gum
- 1 ½ cups cheddar cheese, shredded
- 2 tbsp. garlic powder
- 1 tbsp. parsley
- ½ tbsp. oregano

Directions:

1. Lightly beat eggs and butter together then add to the bread machine pan.

2. Add dry ingredients to the pan.

3. Set the bread to the gluten free setting.

4. When the bread is done, remove bread machine pan from the bread machine.

5. Let cool slightly before transferring to a cooling rack.

6. You can store your bread for up to 5 days.

Nutritional Value Per Serving:

Calories: 142

Carbohydrates: 3g

Protein: 6g

Fat: 13g

Faux Sourdough Bread

Prep time: 10 minutes

Servings: 12

Difficulty: intermediate

Ingredients:

- 2 cups bread flour (white)
- ½ cup plus 1 tablespoon hot water
- ¼ cup sour cream
- 1½ tablespoons butter, melted
- 1 tablespoon apple cider vinegar
- ½ tablespoon sugar
- ½ teaspoon salt
- ¾ teaspoon instant yeast

Directions:

1. Put all ingredients in the bread machine.
2. Set the bread machine to French bread.
3. When ready, remove the bread and allow about 5 minutes to cool the loaf.
4. Put it on a rack to cool it completely

Nutritional Value Per Serving:

Calories: 102

Carbohydrates: 2.5g

Fat: 4g

Protein: 4g

Fiber: 1g

Cranberry Bread

Prep time

Serves: 20

Difficulty: intermediate

Ingredients:

- 2 cups almond flour
- ½ cup erythritol
- 1 ½ tsp baking powder
- ½ tsp baking soda
- 1 tsp salt
- 4 tbsps. coconut oil
- 1 tsp nutmeg, ground
- 4 eggs
- ½ cup coconut milk
- 12 Oz cranberries

Directions:

1. Add wet ingredients to bread machine pan.
2. Add dry ingredients to bread machine pan.
3. Set bread machine to the gluten free setting.
4. When it is ready, remove the pan from the machine.

5. Let cool slightly before transferring to a cooling rack.

6. You can store your bread for up to 5 days.

Nutritional Value Per Serving:

Calories: 127

Carbohydrates: 10g

Protein: 3g

Fat: 11g

Almond Bread with Garlic

Prep time: 4 hours

Servings: 8

Difficulty: intermediate

Ingredients:

- 3 cups of almond flour

- 2 teaspoons dry yeast

- 5 garlic cloves, chopped

- 5 tablespoons Olive oil

- 1 cup of garlic butter, melted

- 2 cups of water

- 2 teaspoons sugar

- 2 egg yolks

- Sea salt to taste

Directions:

1. Melt the unsalted butter by making it softer, by taking it out of the fridge and leaving for around 30 minutes or melt the butter using a frying pan. Meanwhile chop the garlic cloves.

2. Put the almond flour into the bowl and then add in the yeast, sugar, garlic, egg yolks, Olive oil and sea salt and mix until there is a smooth consistency and homogenous mass.

3. Spoon the mixture into the bread machine and add in the water and melted softened garlic butter, mix well.

4. Lubricate the surface of the dough with the water or the egg yolk.

5. Now close the lid and turn the bread machine on the basic/white bread program.

6. After the breakfast wheat bread with garlic is ready, take it out and leave for 1 hour covered with the towel and then you can consume the bread, although we recommend eating your bread after 24 hours.

Nutritional Value Per Serving:

Calories: 190

Fat: 3g

Carbohydrates 5

Sugar 0g

Proteins: 6

Almond Bread with Hazelnuts and Garlic

Prep time: 4 hours

Servings: 8

Difficulty: beginners

Ingredients:

- 3 cups of almond flour

- 2 teaspoons dry yeast

- 1 cup of hazelnuts

- 10 garlic cloves, chopped

- 10 tablespoons Olive oil

- 1 cup of garlic butter, melted

- 2 cups of water

- 2 teaspoons sugar

- 2 egg yolks

- Sea salt to taste

Directions

1. Preheat the oven to 290°-320°Fahrenheit and roast the hazelnuts in the oven for 10-15 minutes until lightly browned and crispy. Set aside to cool completely. Grind the hazelnuts using a food processor.

2. Melt the unsalted butter by making it softer, by taking it out of the fridge and leaving for around 30 minutes or melt the butter using a frying pan. Meanwhile chop the garlic cloves.

3. Put the almond flour into the bowl and then add in the yeast, sugar, garlic, egg yolks, Olive oil and sea salt and mix until there is a smooth consistency and homogenous mass. Add in the hazelnuts.

4. Spoon the mixture into the bread machine and add in the water and melted softened garlic butter, mix well.

5. Lubricate the surface of the dough with the water or the egg yolk.

6. Now close the lid and turn the bread machine on the basic/white bread program.

7. After the breakfast wheat bread with garlic is ready, take it out and leave for 1 hour covered with the towel and then you can consume the bread, although we recommend eating your bread after 24 hours.

Nutritional Value Per Serving:

Calories: 113

Fat: 2g

Carbohydrates 3.9

Sugar 0g

Proteins: 5

Mustard bread

Prep time: 2 hours

Servings: 10

Difficulty: intermediate

Ingredients:

- 1 ¼ cups milk

- 3 tablespoons sunflower oil

- 3 tablespoons sour cream

- 2 tablespoons dry mustard

- 1 egg

- ½ sachet sugar vanilla

- 4 cups (690 g) flour

- 1 teaspoon dry yeast

- 2 tablespoons sugar

- 2 teaspoons salt

Directions

1. Pour the milk and sunflower oil into the bread maker's container, and then add sour cream and egg.

2. Next, pour in flour, salt, sugar, mustard powder, vanilla sugar.

3. Then make a small groove in the flour and sprinkle yeast into it. Close the cover of the bread maker and turn on the

program for the preparation of classic bread; select the desired crustiness of the crust.

4. Then the bread maker will do everything, and you can do your own thing. When the bread is ready, the bread maker will signal.

5. Once the bread is ready, take it out while it's warm. And then cut it into slices and enjoy the taste of real, homemade bread.

Nutritional Value Per Serving:

Calories 140

Fat 9.2g

Carbohydrate 4.6g

Sugars 5.5g

Protein 9.3g

Multigrain Sourdough Bread

Prep time: 10 minutes

Servings: 10

Difficulty: intermediate

Ingredients:

- ⅓ cup plus 1 tablespoon hot water

- ½ cup Simple Sourdough Starter, fed, active, and at room temperature

- 4 teaspoons melted butter, cooled

- 1⅔ tablespoons sugar

- ½ teaspoon salt

- 1 teaspoon bread machine yeast

- ½ cup multigrain cereal

- 1¾ cups bread flour (white)

Directions:

1. Put all ingredients in the bread machine.

2. Program the machine for Whole-Wheat/Whole-Grain bread, select light or medium crust, and press Start.

3. When ready, remove the bread and allow about 5 minutes to cool the loaf.

4. Put it on a rack to cool it completely.

Nutritional Value Per Serving:

Calories: 172

Fat: 2g

Carbohydrates: 3.2g

Fiber: 2g

Protein: 14g

Almond Corn bread

Prep time: 2.5 hours

Servings: 10

Difficulty: intermediate

Ingredients:

- 1 ¼ cups milk

- 2-3 tablespoons vegetable oil

- 3 cups almond flour

- ¾ cup flour corn

- 4 eggs

- 1 tablespoon baking powder

- 1 teaspoon salt

Directions:

1. The recipe for cooking cornbread in a bread maker should start with the combination of all the liquid ingredients. First, pour the milk into the bread maker and add vegetable (or preferably corn) oil.

2. For the next step, add salt. The amount of salt can be adjusted to taste.

3. Now add the baking powder.

4. At this stage, you must mix everything thoroughly to allow the sugar and salt to dissolve well.

5. Then add the eggs.

6. The final stage will be adding wheat and corn flour. The flour must first be sifted.

7. When all the ingredients are already in the bucket, you can send it to the bread maker.

8. After about 2 hours, cornbread in the bread maker will be ready. It should be well cooled and then cut and served to the table.

Nutritional Value Per Serving:

Calories 104

Fat 7.3g

Carbohydrate 4.1g

Sugars 5.1g

Protein 9.6g

Raisin Bran Bread

Prep time: 3 hours

Servings: 10

Difficulty: Expert

Ingredients:

- 1 cup + 1 tablespoon hot water

- 2 tablespoons butter, softened

- ¼ cup packed brown sugar

- 1 ½ cups raisin bran

- ½ teaspoon salt

- ¼ teaspoon baking soda

- 2 ¼ cups bread flour

- 2 ¼ teaspoons active dry yeast

- ½ cup raisins

Directions:

Set the butter out to soften

Put all of the ingredients in your bread machine EXCEPT for the raisins, in the order listed above starting with the water, and finishing with the yeast. Set the bread machine to the basic function.

Check on the dough after about 5 minutes and make sure that it's a soft ball. Add water 1 tablespoon at a time if it's too dry, and add flour 1 tablespoon at a time if it's too wet.

About 5 minutes before the last kneading cycle is finished add in the raisins.

When bread is done allow it cool on a wire rack.

Nutritional Value Per Serving:

Calories: 118

Fiber: 1.5 g

Fat: 1.8 g

Carbohydrates: 3.8 g

Protein: 2.7 g.

Ricotta Bread

Prep time: 3 hours

Servings: 10

Difficulty: intermediate

Ingredients:

- 1/3 cup milk
- 1 cup ricotta cheese
- 2 tablespoons butter
- 1 egg
- 2 ½ tablespoons sugar
- 1 teaspoon salt
- 2 ¼ cups bread flour
- 1 ½ teaspoons yeast

Directions:

1. Put all of the bread ingredients in your bread machine, in the order listed above starting with the milk, and finishing with the yeast.

2. Make a well in middle of the flour and place the yeast in the well. Make sure the well doesn't touch any liquid. Set the bread machine to the basic function with light crust.

3. Check on the dough after about 5 minutes and make sure that it's a soft ball. Add water 1 tablespoon at a time if it's too dry, and add flour 1 tablespoon at a time if it's too wet.

4. When bread is done allow it cool on a wire rack.

Nutritional Value Per Serving:

Calories: 115

Fiber: 1.1 g

Fat: 6.5 g

Carbs: 3.3 g

Protein: 8.5 g.

Sweet Orange Bread

Prep time: 3 hours

Servings: 12

Difficulty: beginners

Ingredients:

Bread:

- ½ cup plus 1 tablespoon water
- 3 tablespoons frozen orange juice concentrate, thawed
- 1 egg
- 3 cups bread flour
- ½ teaspoon grated orange peel
- ¼ cup granulated sugar
- 2 tablespoons instant nonfat dry milk
- 1 ½ tablespoons butter or margarine, softened
- 1 ¼ teaspoons salt
- 2 teaspoons bread machine or quick active dry yeast

Orange Glaze:

- ¾ cups powdered sugar
- 1 tablespoon orange juice

Directions:

1. Set out the butter to soften, and the orange juice concentrate to thaw.

2. Put all of the dough ingredients in your bread machine, in the order listed above, starting with the water and ending with the yeast. Set the bread machine to the basic setting, and medium or light crust.

3. When the bread is done let it cool on a rack.

4. While the bread is cooling, mix the glaze ingredients in a bowl until a smooth glaze is formed. Spread it on the loaf once cooled.

Nutritional Value Per Serving:

Calories: 189

Fiber: 1.0 g

Fat: 2.2 g

Carbs: 3.8.

Protein: 4.3 g.

French Bread

Prep time: 3 hours

Servings: 14

Difficulty: intermediate

Ingredients:

- 1 1/3 cups warm water

- 1 ½ tablespoons olive oil

- 1 ½ teaspoons salt

- 2 tablespoons sugar

- 4 cups all-purpose flour; or bread flour

- 2 teaspoons yeast

Directions:

1. Put the warm water in your bread machine first.

2. Next put in the olive oil, then the salt, and finally the sugar. Make sure to follow that exact order. Then put in the flour, make sure to cover the liquid ingredients.

3. In the center of the flour make a small indentation, make sure the indentation doesn't go down far enough to touch the liquid. Put the yeast in the indentation.

4. Set the bread machine to the French Bread Cycle.

5. After 5 minutes of kneading, check on the dough. If the dough is stiff and dry add ½ - 1 tablespoon of water until the dough becomes a soft ball.

6. If the dough is too wet, add 1 tablespoon of flour until the right consistency is reached. Let the bread cool for 10 minutes before slicing.

Nutritional Value Per Serving:

Calories: 121

Fiber: 1.1 g

Fat: 1.9 g

Carbs: 2.9g

Protein: 3.9 g.

German Black Bread

Prep time: 3 hours 50 minutes

Servings: 10

Difficulty: Expert

Ingredients:

- 1 cup water plus 2 tablespoons water
- 2 tablespoons apple cider vinegar
- 2 tablespoons molasses
- 1 tablespoon sugar
- 1 teaspoon salt
- 1 teaspoon instant coffee
- ¼ teaspoon fennel seeds
- 1 tablespoon caraway seeds
- ½ ounce unsweetened chocolate
- ½ cup bran cereal flakes
- ½ cup bread flour
- ½ cup rye flour
- 2 cups whole almond flour
- 1 package active dry yeast

Directions:

1. Put all of the bread ingredients in your bread machine in the order listed above starting with the water, and finishing with the yeast. Set the bread machine to the whole wheat function.

2. Check on the dough after about 5 minutes and make sure that it's a soft ball. Add water 1 tablespoon at a time if it's too dry, and add flour 1 tablespoon at a time if it's too wet.

3. When bread is done allow it cool on a wire rack.

Nutritional Value Per Serving:

Calories: 102

Carbs: 3.8 g

Fiber: 3.4 g

Fat: 1.4 g

Protein: 5.0 g.

Herb Focaccia Bread

Prep time: 3.5 hours

Servings: 8

Difficulty: Expert

Ingredients:

Dough:

- 1 cup water
- 2 tablespoons canola oil
- 1 teaspoon salt
- 1 teaspoon dried basil
- 3 cups bread flour
- 2 teaspoons bread machine yeast

Topping:

- 1 tablespoon canola oil
- ½ cup fresh basil
- 2 cloves garlic (to taste)
- 2 tablespoons grated parmesan cheese
- 1 pinch salt
- 1 tablespoon cornmeal (optional)

Directions:

1. Put all of the bread ingredients in your bread machine, in the order listed above starting with the water, and finishing with the yeast. Make a well in middle of the flour and place the yeast in the well. Make sure the well doesn't touch any liquid. Set the bread machine to the dough function.

2. Check on the dough after about 5 minutes and make sure that it's a soft ball. Add water 1 tablespoon at a time if it's too dry, and add flour 1 tablespoon at a time if it's too wet.

3. When dough is ready put it on a lightly floured hard surface. Cover the dough and let it rest for 10 minutes.

4. While the dough is resting, chop up the garlic and basil, grease a 13x9 inch pan and evenly distribute cornmeal on top of it.

5. Once the dough has rested, press it into the greased pan. Drizzle oil on the dough and evenly distribute the salt parmesan, garlic, and basil.

Nutritional Value Per Serving:

Calories: 108

Carbs: 37.4 g

Fiber: 1.6 g

Fat: 7.3 g

Protein: 7.7 g.

Chapter 6: Shopping List

Almond flour	Garlic powder	Tartar cream	Orange juice
Baking powder	Onion powder	Sour cream	Orange peel
Xanthan gum	Lemons	Ground nutmeg	Molasses
Cheddar cheese	Erythritol	Ground allspice	Instant coffee
Garlic powder	Cinnamon	Pumpkin puree	Fennel seeds
Parsley	Mozzarella	Zucchini	Caraway seeds
Oregano	Butter	Ginger	Canola oil
Salt	Garlic	Walnuts	multigrain cereal
Chia seeds	Egg yolks	Black olives	Parsley
Pumpkin seeds	Psyllium husk powder	Basil	Parmesan cheese
Flaxseed	Yeast	Sunflower seeds	Thyme
Baking soda	Olive oil	Paprika	Bananas
Coconut oil	Whey protein powder	Cumin	Whole milk
egg whites	Buttermilk	green bell pepper	Vanilla
Almond milk	Apple cider vinegar	Cajun seasoning	Pecans
Coconut flour		Raspberries	Mustard
Ghee		Blueberries	brown sugar
		Himalayan salt	

Eggs	Chia seeds	Cranberries	ricotta cheese
Rosemary	Sesame seeds		Collagen
Sage	Inulin		protein

Conclusion

Thank you for reaching the end of this book. A bread machine and this book is really a perfect couple in your kitchen. Finally, you can have lots of choices of keto bread you can make and serve for your beloved ones.

Bread is staple food that is consumed daily. Since health is the first number of investment in life, it is a good thing if you can prepare it from home. That means everything contained in the bread you and your beloved eat almost every day is under control.

Every recipe in this book is specially created for those who concern not only to health but also taste. However, consume the keto bread with several additional nourishing food, such as vegetables, meat, cheese, and many other healthy food options is totally great since it will enhance the nutritious content of the food.

For sure, every single recipe in this book has been tried in our kitchen and all of them are superb. However, as practice always makes perfect, it is suggested to you to make the bread as often as possible and to engage with your bread machine.

Cutting a lot of foods that are favorites is one of the main struggles that people go through when on keto diet.

Concentrate on the positives and you will succeed. Keto diet helps in prevention of some diseases such as respiratory problems, heart diseases and diabetes.

It does not matter if you want to start the keto lifestyle yourself or you are in search of traditional bread, there are suitable recipes for your every need. They range from sweet to savory and they are healthy and so satisfying. There is little effort needed to make these recipes using the bread machine.

Have wonderful and amazing experiences with your bread machine and enjoy baking, healthy people!

A Cookbook with the 50 Best Low-Carb Keto Bread Recipes to Enhance Weight Loss

Katie Simmons

Text Copyright

Legal & Disclaimer

Upon using the contents and information contained in this book, you agree to hold harmless the Author from and against any damages, costs, and expenses, including any legal fees potentially resulting from the application of any of the information provided by this book. This disclaimer applies to any loss, damages or injury caused by the use and application, whether directly or indirectly, of any advice or information presented, whether for breach of contract, tort, negligence, personal injury, criminal intent, or under any other cause of action.

You agree to accept all risks of using the information presented inside this book.

You agree that by continuing to read this book, where appropriate and/or necessary, you shall consult a professional (including but not limited to your doctor, attorney, or financial advisor or such other advisor as needed) before using any of the suggested remedies, techniques, or information in this book.

Introduction

Bread is a common staple all over the world. Each country has its own special type of bread, so why cut this particular food item out of your diet? Just because you're following the keto diet doesn't mean that you have to stop eating this delicious food. However, you will have to change the types of bread you choose to eat when following this diet.

Keto bread is low in carbs, gluten, and sugar. You can eat lot of it without having to worry about too much sugar or even adding your weight. This is because the flours that make the keto bread lack the regular carbs present in grain flours like wheat.

Since the keto diet consists of foods that are low-carb, high-fat, and moderate in proteins, this means that you have to choose the foods you eat carefully. If you don't want to have to say goodbye to bread forever, you can either choose keto-friendly versions or, better yet, make your own bread. To start off, let's take a look at some of the basic ingredients used in keto baking.

While traditional breads are made with yeast and dairy products, you will find that the substitutions that are used for these keto recipes mimic the chewy and spongy that are found in original recipes. They taste even better and will keep you full.

In this book ill be sharing with you about the varieties of bread that can be enjoyed on keto.

When on a keto lifestyle, you will enjoy the best recipes while you lose weight effortlessly. Who wouldn't want that? I know you want it. This is the reason why you should go for keto bread and enjoy its full benefits. Once you get used to the keto bread, you will never want to eat the other bread because it is sweet and at the same time has several other benefits that come with ketogenic diet.

Chapter 1: Guide to Low Carb Flours and Sweeteners For Baking

Flours

Flour is an important ingredient for baking. However, most types of flour used in non-keto recipes are high in carbohydrates. The good news is that there are some keto-friendly flour alternatives which you can use for your recipes including the following:

Coconut Flour

This type of flour is a by-product of coconut milk. After coconut milk is extracted, coconut meat is left. This is then dried before being finely ground to produce coconut flour - a fine powder which has a similar appearance to wheat flour. Keep in mind that when you use coconut flour, the recipe must also have a lot of eggs or liquids to add moisture to the final product. Coconut flour is an excellent flour substitute if you're allergic to nuts.

Moreover, eggs play a significant role when it comes to baking with coconut flour. Eggs are a binding factor for the ingredients giving a good structure. Failing to use eggs will lead to poor cohesion and ultimately causing your meal to crumble. Use an egg for every quarter cup of coconut flour to get a suitable binding effect.

Coconut flour has a tendency of absorbing liquid quickly. For this reason, you will have to use a little more than the usual recipe. Please do not submerge everything like you trying to replicate some flooded amazon jungle! Lastly you will have to sift the coconut because it can get a bit coarse or clumpy.

Golden Flax Meal

This type of flour is made from finely ground flax seeds. Although it works well in different types of keto baking recipes, it's important to note that it's a heavy type of flour.

Sesame Seed Flour

This is made from finely-ground sesame seeds, and it's another great nut-free alternative. This type of flour isn't very common, but you can make it yourself at home from scratch. Sesame seed flour also has a strong taste so be careful when using this as a replacement in recipes.

Hazelnut Flour

This kind of flour comes from finely ground hazelnuts, and it's an excellent alternative to almond flour. It's less grainy thus producing baked goods with a finer texture. Because of this, hazelnut flour is especially nice in cake and cookie recipes. However, it's one of the more expensive types of low-carb flour options.

Almond Flour and Almond Meal

Almond flour has a light color and texture as it's made from peeled almonds which are finely ground. Before grinding, the almonds are blanched, making it easier to remove the skins. Almond meal looks a lot like almond flour, but the difference is that it has brown-colored flecks in it. This is because almond meal is made from unpeeled almonds. In terms of cost, almond flour is more expensive since it undergoes the blanching process making the production process more labor-intensive.

Sunflower Seed Flour

This is another great alternative for those who are allergic to nuts. Sunflower seed flour is made from ground sunflower seeds. It has a pretty strong taste that varies from one band to another. Therefore, you may have to try out different brands before finding one that you really like.

Sweeteners

Swerve Granular Sweetener

It is also an excellent choice as a blend. It's made from non-digestible carbs sourced from starchy root veggies and select fruits. Start with 3/4 of a tsp for every one of sugar. Increase the portion to your liking. Swerve also has its own confectioners or powdered sugar for your baking needs. On the downside, it is more expensive.

Stevia

Stevia drops include English toffee, hazelnut, vanilla, and chocolate flavors. Stevia is a common herb known as sugar leaf and is available in drops, glycerite, or in powder form. Enjoy making a satisfying cup of sweetened coffee or other favorite drink. Some individuals think the stevia drops are too bitter. At first, use only three drops to equal one tsp of sugar.

Erythritol

This was discovered by chemist John Stenhouse in 1848. The substance occurs naturally in some fruits and mushrooms. It is produced industrially by subjecting starch from corn to enzymatic hydrolysis to yield glucose, which is then fermented using fungus to produce erythritol. This has been used in Japan since the 1990s. It comes in crystal and powdered form, with the latter being more commonly preferred.

It has good taste with minimal aftertaste, and has mild cooling effect on the mouth. It has 0.2 calories per gram, which is 5% the calories of sugar, with 65% sweetness.

Allulose (Psicose)

It is a sugar which has low calorie levels but just as sweet and clean as the expected of sugar.

The existence of allulose is very little in nature because it is available in small volumes. Allulose was found in wheat at first and later on in some particular fruits which included raisins, figs and jackfruit.

For sweet foods such as brown sugar, maple syrup and caramel sauce, allulose occurs in little quantities.

Allulose is a simple sugar (monosaccharide) and the body absorbs it automatically and it is calorie free.

It is ideal for people who want to limit their calorie intake. People do that by taking drinks and foods with low ingredients with low calorie sweeteners like allulose. This is also made possible by the fact that allulose replicates the technical sugar functions in some foods like baked foods and ice cream.

Xylitol

In its refined form, xylitol is a white crystalline substance that resembles table sugar. It comes from the birch tree and is thus classified as a tree sugar, in the same way that maple sugar comes from the maple tree.

What sets this sugar substitute apart is that it has a chemical structure that actually helps the teeth. With table sugar, a fermentation process occurs in the mouth when the saliva dissolves the sugar. Fermentation commonly occurs with wine and other beverages that you want to age. In fermentation, sugar is broken down into an acidic compound because of certain bacteria.

Stevia

Stevia is an aromatic herb originating from South America, especially from Brazil and Paraguay, which has been used since ancient times as a sweetener as well as a medicine in these countries. Stevia is a natural sweetener derived from the leaves of the Stevia rebaudiana plant. It has no calories or carbohydrates and zero glycemic index so it's often used to reduce or replace sugar in recipes. That said, it's about ten to fifteen times sweeter than other natural sweeteners so it doesn't take much stevia to sweeten a recipe. It can also have a slightly bitter aftertaste depending on how it's used and it doesn't caramelize like other sweeteners, so it works best in small amounts and in recipes where there are other sources of sweetness, such as honey, maple syrup, or fruit. The sweetness also varies by brand.

Stevia carries some health benefits, rather than just risks. These include;

  i. Positive side effects claimed for Stevia include:

  ii. Helps balance blood sugar

  iii. Sweeter than sugar

  iv. Improves digestion

  v. Increases energy levels

  vi. Can be used to speed healing

Chapter 2: The Keto Bread demystified

Bread ingredients

There are many keto breads for you to bake at home. As a result, there are many varying recipes of keto breads for you to pick from. This probes one question if you give some thought into it. What qualifies a given type of bread as keto bread if so? Although there are many existing recipes of keto breads, there is a given type of consistency in their ingredients. Other ingredients are secondary but a given few are recognized as the building blocks of keto bread.

1. Butter

It is milk fat thus a dairy product. Butter has saturated fats and a higher concentration of calories compared to proteins and carbohydrates. It is very versatile ingredient regardless of the recipe. It can be used in cooking, spreading and baking.

There are also different types of butter used in keto diet. They are clarified butter, grass-fed butter and ghee. Clarified butter is entirely fat without lactose, milk or protein. It is good for an individual who is lactose intolerant. Ghee takes a bit longer to prepare compared to clarified butter. Existing milk solids in it are browned and if kept well, can take a long time before going bad.

Grass-fed butter is the best since it contains higher levels of Conjugated Linoleic Acid compared to commercial butter. This is as a result of the feed given to the cows when owner opts for grass rather than commercial feed. Conjugated Linoleic Acid assists consumers in losing body fat.

When it comes to butter in keto diet, there are specific known brands which are highly recommended. They are Kerrygold, Allgau, Organic Valley and Smjor. You will find them in many keto recipes today for they are grass-fed butter. However, Kerrygold does use commercial feed as substitute for their cow feed in winters. Even so, some of their grass-fed butter would still be available.

2. Flour

When baking your keto bread, you can either opt for Almond flour, Almond meal, ground flaxseed, flax meal or coconut flour. Almond flour is obtained from ground almond seeds. In addition to this, Almond flour and Almond meal are two different things. The former involving the removal of the skins while the latter is prepared whole (skins and seeds). It is possible to produce your own almond flour at home. This type of flour is more nutritious than wheat flour being rich in fibers and healthy fats. It is a low-carb and good for baking.

Coconut flour is another alternative to the wheat flour. It is produced from coconut pulp after the raw product has been processed for its milk. Rich in proteins, healthy fats and fiber, coconut flour is good for baking. However, its high fiber concentration makes it denser than regular flour meaning you will have to work with a given ratio. When working on a given recipe requiring you to substitute wheat flour for coconut flour, the ratio will be 1:4. For a cup of regular wheat, you will substitute it with only a quarter cup of coconut flour.

Moreover, eggs play a significant role when it comes to baking with coconut flour. Eggs are a binding factor for the ingredients giving a good structure. Failing to use eggs will lead to poor cohesion and ultimately causing your meal to crumble. Use an egg for every quarter cup of coconut flour to get a suitable binding effect.

Coconut flour has a tendency of absorbing liquid quickly. For this reason you will have to use a little more than the usual recipe. Please do not submerge everything like you trying to replicate some flooded amazon jungle! Lastly you will have to sift the coconut because it can get a bit coarse or clumpy.

Macadamia nuts and flax seeds are other two sources of keto flour. Flaxseeds are rich in dietary fiber and omega 3-fats. When consumed whole (skins and seeds) they are known as flax meal.

3. Sweeteners

Sweeteners can be opted as a substitute for sugar. Contrary though, not all sweeteners are low-carb ones. In fact, there are some sweeteners which contain more carb content than sugar. Honey, a natural sweetener, has more carb content than sugar.

Furthermore, there are sweeteners that can work for some people while others it may result in digestive issues. Xylitol is a good example of such sweeteners. It is a sugar alcohol which may not be a great sugar substitute for every individual in your household. Apart from this, Xylitol can increase blood sugar levels in other persons too.

The sweeteners you can use for baking are stevia, Erythritol and Monk fruit sweetener. They neither bring digestive complications nor increase your blood sugar levels. In addition to this, they are low-carb sweeteners. Although they are versatile and can be used in any recipe, they do have different ratios upon substituting with sugar.

Stevia and Monk fruit sweetener are natural sweeteners as they are obtained from plants. However, some people state that Stevia has a rather bitter aftertaste. On the other hand, Monk fruit sweetener has no aftertaste to it.

Erythritol is a sugar alcohol produced after fermentation of corn or birch. It is 70% to 80% identical to sugar thus you have to compensate more to get the expected sweetness. It has a cooling effect similar to mint but this shouldn't make you worry.

4. Yeast

You will find that the active ingredient in any bread product is going to be the yeast. When properly activated, it will create carbon dioxide that is required for the bread to grow in size. This is due to the air pockets that are created by the carbon dioxide which are held in by the stretchy properties of the dough itself.

You cannot see it, but the carbon dioxide reproduces multiple thousands of times in each bread product. It is why the bread will grow noticeably larger in size when left to properly rise before and during baking.

Before the baking process, you will see the largest difference in the expansion of the bread. This process continues when heat is applied after the initial rising process. While the bread is baking, it permanently traps the carbon dioxide that was trapped in the dough and grows a little larger and will keep its shape after being removed from the heat.

You will find that the bread loaves will have larger air pockets in comparison to muffins. This is due to the different textures of the bread products. This is why it is harder to get bread loaves to rise versus smaller items such as biscuits and muffins.

Dry Active Yeast

This is used in a couple of the recipes and requires the most patience. These recipes may pop out to you as they include the ingredient of honey. Before you think that I have made a mistake, honey is purposefully mixed with the yeast so that it can properly activate. The yeast requires the sugars that are present in the honey to create the needed carbon dioxide to perform the rising capabilities.

Through the baking process, this sugar is burned off, much like the process involved with cooking with alcohol. You know that the yeast is doing its job when it starts to froth in the bowl after the 7 minutes has passed for it to activate.

If you have problems with the yeast bubbling, it is due to the water not being the correct temperature. If you have the water hotter than 110° Fahrenheit, then you have actually killed the yeast preventing it from activating. If the water is cooler than 105°, then it is not hot enough to activate the yeast in the first place. Both of the results mean you need to start the process of warming the water yet again. Avoid having to repeat the steps by having a kitchen thermometer handy to ensure this finicky component will work properly. You will find that this process takes much longer than the other more common ingredient used in leavening bread.

5. Baking Soda

You may remember science class where you had the replica of the volcano where you had baking soda and red food coloring inside and poured simple vinegar inside the well. Immediately the volcano erupted with all the red lava glory.

This is what is happening with your bread on a smaller and much less messy scale. As you can see from this illustration, the baking soda used in the Keto diet breads have a much quicker rising process and does not need to be monitored as in the case of the dry active yeast. This is why this is the preferred way of modern bread making.

Bread machines

As you can see, there are so many ingredients you can use for your baking (and cooking) while on this diet. As long as you have these basic ingredients in your kitchen, you can stick with it long-term. Apart from the basic ingredients, there are also a number of basic tools you would need for keto baking. Some of these basic tools include the following:

- Baking sheets

- Cake pans

- Cookie scoops

- Cooling racks

- Food processor

- Hand mixer

- Loaf pans

- Measuring bowls (made of stainless steel)

- Measuring cups

- Measuring spoons

- Parchment paper

- Rolling pins

- Silicone baking mats

- Spatulas

- Stand-up mixer

- Whisks

Start off with a few basic tools and you can begin building your baking arsenal over time so you can create more complex recipes which require additional ingredients.

Homemade bread

When you're starting on the keto diet and you plan to bake your own bread, it's helpful for you to know the most basic keto bread recipe. The great thing about keto baking is that there are so many food items you can create using simple ingredients - and a lot of the recipes (as you will see later on) have similar ingredients. This means that if you really plan to do a lot of baking, there are certain ingredients that you may want to consider buying in bulk as you will be using them for different recipes.

When it comes to keto baking, it is ideal for you to start off with the simplest, easiest recipes so you can get the hang of the whole process. This allows you to familiarize yourself with the basic keto-friendly ingredients before you start creating more elaborate dishes.

Properties of bread

The major property of the keto bread is that it is low in carbs. This is what makes it keto.

Bread can be eaten during breakfast or any time of the day as a snack or a dessert. It is popular because it can be made and eaten several times.

Preparation

If you don't have baking powder, you can invent your own by including baking soda and lemon juice or citric acid. The ratio of baking soda to citric acid is 2:1. For lemon juice you will go with 2 tbsps for a single tsp of baking soda. However, don't change the quantities if the recipe has already provided it for you. Always make sure to directly add lemon juice on the baking soda for it to react well. You may opt to do this on the side before mixing all the ingredients.

When you're starting on the keto diet and you plan to bake your own bread, it's helpful for you to know the most basic keto bread recipe. The great thing about keto baking is that there are so many food items you can create using simple ingredients - and a lot of the recipes (as you will see later on) have similar ingredients. This means that if you really plan to do a lot of baking, there are certain ingredients that you may want to consider buying in bulk as you will be using them for different recipes.

When it comes to keto baking, it is ideal for you to start off with the simplest, easiest recipes so you can get the hang of the whole process. This allows you to familiarize yourself with the basic keto-friendly ingredients before you start creating more elaborate dishes.

Leavening of bread

Leaving is the process where gas is added to the dough when baking to make the bread or what is being baked or prepared to rise. Leavening of bread is very important in baking.

There are different leavening agents which produce air that makes the bread to rise. These different agents produce air in different ways.

There are thee major kinds of leavening agent. They are steam, chemical and biological.

Chapter 3: Keto bread tips and FAQs

Keto Bread Tips

Baking Tips

Do not get frustrated if a dish does not turn out perfectly as you are baking with new ingredients which are usually fussy and will take some practice. However, read through these tips carefully to gain the knowledge that you will require to have your Keto breads turn out to be a success!

Temperature is everything

You want to use eggs, cream cheese, sour cream, milk and any other cooled items set at room temperature. This is due to cold items not mixing particularly well into the almond and coconut flours which are used in Keto and if they are not brought down to room temperature, then your bread will not properly rise.

A trick for the eggs, in particular, is to use a bowl of warm water to immerse the eggs for the duration of 4 minutes. This will quickly bring them to room temperature which is a nice trick in case you forgot to pull them out of the fridge.

Make sure that you measure your ingredients properly

This will lead to consistent results for all the Keto recipes that you find. The correct method in measuring is to spoon the ingredient into the cup rather than scooping it out of the bag directly. This will create perfect results every time as you will not over pack the ingredients using this method. You can also ensure that all the ingredients are the correct increments if you purchase a simple kitchen or baking scale.

Ensure the yeast is properly proofed

Not every recipe includes dry active yeast. However, for the ones that do, there is a specific process to follow as outlined in those particular recipes. It includes combining the yeast with honey for the yeast to feed upon. Do not worry about the sugar content as the honey is for the yeast to feed upon, creating the carbon dioxide required for the bread to rise. The sugar will be cooked off during the process and will not be present in the final result.

Once combined, you will blend water which is the specific temperature of 105° - 110° which can be checked with a kitchen thermometer or it will be slightly warm to the touch. You will know that this process was successful by the mixture becoming bubbly after waiting for a period of 7 minutes.

If there are no bubbles, simply repeat the process with the correct temperature water. You will not waste a whole dish because this occurs at the beginning of the recipe.

Temperature is important during the rising process

You want to keep your rising bread in an environment where the temperature is not going to vary much and will be undisturbed during the rising time. You want to have the area to be slightly warm and humid, but not hot as this will stop the rising process. It is suggested to keep the covered tray on top of the stove which is preheating.

Always Sift Your Coconut Flour:

Not sifting your coconut flour will result in a grainy bread full of coconut flour clumps…yuck! To sift your coconut flour, simply use a mesh strainer, and add the coconut flour. Sift over a large container or bowl.

Keep away from xylitol

When using any yeast in your recipes, you want to make sure that xylitol is not an additive in your ingredients as it rapidly decreases the rising of the dough and will cause them to become flat. You will find that Monk Fruit and Erythritol do not contain xylitol and may be used as a substitute for sweeteners that have this additive included.

Loaf pan size is important

There are a wide variety of baking pans out there. I have made it easy by including the particular pan that is required for each recipe. However, if you do not have that specific size, always opt to go with a pan that is the next size up rather than downsizing. This will ensure that the dough will not rise too far causing the bread to burst over the pan.

The measurements for pans are calculated from the top of the pan and does not include the pan itself.

Pure ingredients are everything

Especially when dealing with the different varieties of cheese, you want to make sure there are no preservatives or additives. Also, opt for the skim or whole milk types as these will have less water to weep during the baking process.

When baking powder is being used, it is a priority to ensure that it is as fresh as possible. Since there is no gluten present, it needs to be of the best quality to make the rising process work properly.

Not sure if your baking powder is still active? Do a small test by combining with boiling water. If bubbles occur immediately, then your baking powder will make your bread properly rise.

A perfect way to grease any pan

If you want to make sure that you do not run into the problem of your Keto breads sticking to the pan, this fail-proof trick will take the headache out of baking. Dissolve 2 tsps. of coconut oil in a saucepan and then apply to your pan with a pastry brush. Set in the freezer for a minimum of 20 minutes as the oil hardens. Pull out of the freezer before filling with your dough.

Separating the eggs is a necessary step

It may seem like a pain at the time, but there is a reason that you will find the eggs are separated. This simple measure also helps the Keto breads to rise. When incorporating the whipped eggs into the batter, do not over mix. This is due to you counteracting the airiness that has been created by whipping the eggs and your breads will not rise properly.

For the bread loaves

If you find that your bread is crumbling when you are slicing, ensure the loaf is completely cooled. This will help the bread to set and firm up more when given the time to come to room temperature.

For the muffins

If you are having trouble with your muffins rising properly, add a combination of baking soda and vinegar which causes the carbon dioxide reaction required for proper rising. You will also find that many of the recipes already incorporate this trick.

Tips for the cookies

Different people enjoy cookies hard or soft. Luckily there is a trick in Keto baking which lets you have a choice. The biggest trick is to have the treats completely cool so that the cookie will not crumble.

If you like to have softer cookies, leave them on the countertop in a lidded container or cookie jar. They will keep fresh for up to 5 days. Refrigerate the cookies after they are completely cooled in a covered tub and they will become harder. They will keep for up to 7 days this way.

If your cookies are not rising the way you prefer, simply combine a half tsp of apple cider vinegar while blending the batter. You will find some of the recipes already utilize this trick.

For the Bagels:

Coconut creates bagels that are denser. On the other hand, almond flour creates a light bagel. You can substitute whichever flour for the result that you prefer.

Tips for Saving Time

The keto diet doesn't have to be either complicated or difficult. Although more and more keto-friendly products and food items are being made available these days, it's always better to cook your meals and bake goods at home. Though it might seem odd at the beginning, once you get the hang of things, this process will become faster, easier, and more enjoyable. Since this book is all about baking, here are some time-saving tips for you:

Make riced cauliflower in bulk then use airtight containers to freeze it. That way, you can simply take the amount you need when your recipe calls for it.

For recipes that call for boiled low-carb food items, use an instant pot. This allows you to cook ingredients in bulk faster.

Stock up on parchment paper as you can use this to line your baking sheets, pans, and other similar items before placing them in the oven.

Use your freshly-baked bread loaves to make scrumptious sweet or savory sandwiches. Then store these in the refrigerator for meals on-the-go.

When planning which recipes to bake, check the ingredients to see if they share common items. This makes shopping a lot easier, especially if you want to make meal prepping part of your keto journey.

Tips for Saving Money

Apart from saving time, there are also things you can do in order to save money while following the keto diet. Starting a new diet is always challenging, no matter what type of diet you choose to follow. Most of the time, you won't even know where to start. Although you've already learned all that you can about the diet, actually taking the first step towards starting it can be very intimidating.

If you want to stick with your keto journey, then you must make sure that you don't break the bank just because of it. Otherwise, you might end up deciding that the diet isn't working for you since you're losing money on it. This doesn't have to be the case! To help you out, here are some clever money-saving tips you can try:

Create things from scratch

Whether you're baking pastries or cooking dishes, it's important to learn how to create things from scratch. Although it's easier and more convenient to purchase ready-made, prepackaged keto food products, doing so will surely make you lose a lot of money. If you want to stick with your budget, learning how to make homemade meals from scratch is of the essence.

Purchase fresh, whole ingredients

Buying ingredients which are fresh and whole allows you to whip up healthy meals and snacks that fit right into your keto diet. In fact, a proper keto diet should be built around these types of ingredients so you can get high-quality sources of macros and the rest of the nutrients. Also, fresh and whole ingredients are a lot cheaper which means that you can save a lot of money.

Buy local produce, which is in season

Do research on which foods and food items are available each season. Purchasing local produce that is in season allows you to get the ingredients you need at an affordable price. As long as you know which ingredients are in season in your locale, you can start planning your meals and recipes easily and more effectively.

Buy ingredients in bulk

Speaking of saving money on ingredients, buying in bulk also allows you to save some money. Go around your locale and check out all the food shops, supermarkets, farmer's markets, and convenience stores. That way, you can determine which places offer the freshest ingredients, which ones have the best prices, and which places offer bulk or wholesale products.

Bake (and cook) in bulk

Of course, if you buy in bulk, it's a good idea to use these ingredients in bulk too. This is where meal prepping comes in. Once a week, set aside some time to plan your meals, shop for all of the ingredients and bake/cook all of your meals for the whole week. This is an excellent way to save money and ensure that you don't feel tempted to buy takeout or ready-made foods, which are less healthy and more expensive.

The bottom line is this: when you start the keto diet, keep in mind that this involves a lot of planning. All of these tips can help make your journey easier so you don't have to feel like you're being constantly challenged. When you see how much time and money you're saving, this can even become your motivation to stick with the diet long-term.

Although starting the low-carb keto diet may help you lose weight, there are some things for you to consider. First of all, if you really want to shed those unwanted pounds and enjoy all of the health benefits the keto diet has to offer, you must follow it properly. As stated previously, this diet does come with restrictions and you should make sure that you follow them religiously.

Also, to stay on the safe side, you may want to consult with your doctor before you start this diet. This is especially true for people who are suffering from medical conditions or for those who have a complicated medical history. If you've already made the decision to go low-carb, here are some pointers for you:

Choose your carbs wisely

The main energy sources of the body come from simple and complex carbs. Simple carbs are those naturally found in milk and fruits, but sweets such as candies also contain them. When choosing foods which contain carbs, opt for the complex variety such as starchy veggies, lentils, beans, and legumes.

Opt for lean protein

Just because you're allowed to eat moderate amounts of protein while on the keto diet, this doesn't mean that you should eat all kinds of protein. If you want to lose weight and improve your health, then the best protein choices are eggs, beans, skinless turkey or chicken breast, and fish.

Make it a habit to read food labels

This allows you to choose the ingredients and food items which fit into your diet more effectively. When you read food labels, this gives you information about the food items you plan to purchase from stores.

Consume a lot of non-starchy veggies and fruits

Although these food items may contain simple carbs, that doesn't mean you should stop eating them. Fruits and veggies are the healthiest kinds of foods, so continue eating them as part of your diet to ensure your overall health.

Plan your meals

Meal planning can be your friend when you're following the keto diet. This involves planning your meals for a specific amount of time (like for one week), shopping for ingredients, then setting one day each week to cook all of the meals you've planned. It's an excellent way to save time, money, and to stick with your diet.

Maintain open communication with your doctor

Finally, it's important to maintain open communication with your doctor, especially when you experience any changes because of the diet. Whether you're at the peak of your health or you're suffering from any kind of medical condition, keeping your doctor in the loop is essential.

Learn How to Check Nutritional Information

As mentioned, it's important to check food labels. In fact, you should make this a habit if you decide to start the keto diet. The good news is that all of the big food companies have introduced new nutrition labels which makes it easier to learn the nutritional information of the foods you plan to buy. Here are some steps to follow when checking nutritional information:

Check the serving size

This information tells you how many calories and nutrients you would get for each serving of the food item. When you know this, you can compare this serving size with the amount you actually consume.

Check the caloric information

This information tells you the amount of energy you obtain for each serving.

Check the percent daily value

This information tells you the percentage of nutrients on a scale which, in turn, tells you if the food item contains minimal or high amounts of nutrients. A DV of 5% and below is considered little and a DV of 15% and above is considered a lot.

Search for these nutrients

Look for calcium, fiber, iron, vitamin A, and vitamin C.

Conversely, try to avoid these

Cholesterol, fat, saturated fat, sodium, and trans fat.

The great thing about nutrition labels is these make it easier to compare products, they allow you to find out the nutritional value of food items, and they help you determine whether or not different food items are appropriate for your diet.

FAQs

What is the difference between a ketogenic diet and a low-carb diet?

Low carb diet is a general term used to describe any diet containing 130 to 150 grams on the total. However ketogenic diets are the subset of this general diet plan. It further restricts the amount of carbohydrate to minimum levels and at the same time requires an increased intake of fat. Thus, a ketogenic diet plan is more specific than the low carbohydrate plan.

Do I need to count calories? Are calories of importance?

Keeping track of caloric intake is important as it directly relates to weight gain. Whether on a low carb diet or on a high one, it is necessary to keep check of the calories.

How can a person track carb intake/ macro?

Whenever you follow a recipe, look for its contents and the nutritional value available with the recipe. If it is not available, look for online nutrition calculators which enables you to calculate the nutritional value within few minutes.

What is the time taken to get to ketosis?

If you are a person of discipline and routine then it typically takes two to three days to start a keto routine. However, it is a gradual process and goes through different stages. Exercise helps boosts the speed of the process. For people with sedentary lifestyles, it can also take weeks.

Can I eat dairy?

This is perhaps the most frequently asked question by the people who are new to a keto diet. Not all dairy products are keto friendly as raw dairy products are high in carbs. But those fermented or processed loses their carbohydrates and are good to use, these include butter, cheese and yoghurt.

Can I eat peanuts?

Not all legumes are not keto friendly, peanuts are one of them. There is a great misconception that peanuts can be taken on a keto diet, but it is clearly not true as they are low on carbs and high in fats. When taken in small amounts, they do not disrupt the balance of the ketogenic diet.

Is ketosis bad?

There is no proven evidence which could suggest that ketosis is dangerous. Many people confuse ketosis with the ketoacidosis, the latter is a health problem which only occurs in patients with diabetes type 1. During ketoacidosis, the ketones level in the blood exceeds up to a critical value. Ketosis, on the other hand, is completely normal and doesn't pose any danger to a person's health.

Are the high-fat foods healthy? Does eating a lot of fat make people fat?

Most of us believe that high fats are unhealthy but it is nothing but a myth. Fats can only be unhealthy if taken with the high amount of carbohydrates. However, when taken with low carbs or no carbs, these fats become a direct and active source of energy for the body. They easily break down and releases essential compounds including ketones.

Can I go off of the ketogenic diet plan and still keep the weight off?

Unfortunately, when you see-saw on any diet plan, you're going to gain the weight back. Some individuals don't understand that you're making a lifestyle change.

188

Do I have to fast while on the ketogenic diet plan?

It's not a requirement. If you ease into the process of fasting as described in this book, you can lower your carbohydrates slowly. Although, if you add the intermittent fasting plan as described, you can also accelerate your weight loss, help hunger control, and cravings as well as detoxification.

Chapter 4: Keto Bread Recipes

Bread

Ketogenic Banana Bread

Prep minutes 10 / Cook 40 minutes / Serves 4/ 355ºF/ Serves: 4

Difficulty: Beginner

PER SEVING: Calories: 164; Fat: 14g; Saturated Fat: 4g; Protein: 6g; Carbohydrates: 4g; Sodium: 121mg; Fiber: 1g; Sugar: 1g

Ingredients

5 eggs

2 tbsps. carbquik

3 tsps. baking powder

1 cup chopped pecans

1 tbsp vanilla sugar-free syrup

¾ cup granular Splenda

3 tsps. banana extract

Directions

Put all ingredients in a blender mixing on HIGH once every addition.

Ensure that the pecans are finely blended as they will be the "flour".

Add the batter in an 8x4" loaf pan which is lubricated. Bake for 40 minutes at 355°F-.

Cool on a rack before serving.

Seeded Bread Loaf

Prep 10 minutes / Cook 50 minutes / Serves 20/ 340ºF

Difficulty: Intermediate

PER SEVING: Calories: 161; Fat: 12.7g; Saturated Fat: 2.1g; Protein: 6.5g; Carbohydrates: 3.6g; Sodium: 56mg; Fiber: 3g; Sugar: 2g;

Ingredients

1 ½ cup almond flour

1 cup sunflower seeds

½ cup chia seeds

½ tsp salt

1 cup pumpkin seeds

2 tbsps. olive oil

1 cup sesame seeds

5 eggs, preferably farm-raised

Directions

Preheat the oven to 340°F.

Place the almond flour and the eggs in a food processor and blend once.

To this, add the seeds, olive oil, and salt and pulse the mixture again until the seeds are broken down into small bits. Don't blend the dough for too long, as the bread won't be crunchy.

Next, line the loaf pan with parchment paper and transfer the dough into it. Shape as needed.

Now, bake the bread 48 to 50 minutes or until the top portion is lightly browned.

Allow the bread to cool completely before slicing. Tip: slice it thinly as the bread is dense.

You can serve the bread either by toasting it with butter or as a base for fried eggs.

Prep 12 minutes/ Cook 12 minutes / Serves 4/ 350°F

Difficulty: Intermediate

PER SEVING: Calories: 307; Fat: 11g; Saturated Fat: 2.1g; Protein: 4g; Carbohydrates: 4g; Sodium: 408mg; Fiber: 0.7g; Sugar: 0g

Ingredients

½ cup coconut flour

1 tsp baking powder

¼ tsp salt

6 eggs (lightly beaten)

½ cup butter(melted)

Directions

Preheat oven to 350°F. spray Associate in Nursing 8" x 4" loaf pan with slippery change of state spray and put aside.

In a small bowl, mix coconut flour, baking powder, and salt until thoroughly combined and set aside.

In a large bowl, beat eggs with an electric hand mixer until frothy. Continue beating and slowly add butter to eggs in a thin stream and beat until thoroughly combined. Continue beating and add dry ingredients to egg mixture and beat until thoroughly combined.

Pour batter into ready 8 x 4" pan and bake for 45 minutes. Let bread cool in pan on a wire rack for 10 minutes. Remove bread from pan to cool completely and slice to serve. Enjoy!

Prep 15 minutes / Cook 30 12 minutes / Serves 1/ 356ºF

Difficulty: Expert

PER SERVING: Calories 348, Total Fat 9.5g, Saturated Fat 4.4g, Sodium 768mg, Total Carbohydrate 70.6g, Dietary Fiber 51.3g, Sugars 0.4g, Protein 12.3g,

Ingredients

5.3-ounce (50g) coconut flour

5 eggs

2 tsps. baking powder

1 tsp salt

5 tbsps. psyllium husk

250ml hot water

Directions

Using a mixing bowl first put your coconut flour. Add psyllium husk, baking powder, salt and mix the contents in the bowl.

Add eggs into the bowl and mix. The content at this point will be less workable but don't worry about it.

Add the hot water and work on the mixture thoroughly.

Align your baking tray with baking paper. Make a focaccia shape out of the dough, put it on the baking tray and make lateral cuts on the dough.

Add olives on top. Sprinkle some rosemary and salt in the cuts.

For 30min, bake it at 356ºF. The center of the bread shouldn't be spongy when you remove it. That's how you know it's ready. You can serve it with butter then or use tomatoes, cheese, avocadoes etc. when it's cool.

Garlic Cheese Bread Loaf

Prep 12 minutes/ Cook 50 minutes / Serves 10/ 355°F

Difficulty: Intermediate

PER SERVING: Calories: 299; Fat: 3g; Saturated Fat: 1g; Protein: 11g; Carbohydrates: 4g; Sodium: 121mg; Fiber: 1g; Sugar: 0g

Ingredients

1 tbsp. parsley seasoning

0.5 cup butter, unsalted and softened

2 tbsp garlic powder

6 large eggs

0.5 tbsp oregano seasoning

1 tsp baking powder, gluten-free

2 cup almond flour

0.5 tsp xanthan gum

1 cup cheddar cheese, shredded

0.5 tsp salt

Directions

Set your stove to heat at the temperature of 355°F.

Utilize baking lining to cover a 9 x 5-inch bread loaf pan

pan and set to the side.

Use a food blender to pulse the eggs until smooth. Combine the butter and pulse for an additional 60 seconds until integrated.

Blend the almond flour and baking powder for approximately 90 more seconds until the batter thickens.

Finally combine the oregano, garlic, parsley, and cheese until integrated.

Distribute into the prepped pan and smooth evenly with a scraper.

For approximately 45 minutes, heat the bread and check with a utensil to ensure it has baked properly when it comes out without residue.

Transfer to the countertop and wait about 15 minutes before slicing and serving.

Herbed Bread Loaf

Prep 10 minutes /Cook 60 minutes /Serves 12/ 350°F

Difficulty: Expert

PER SERVING: Calories: 127; Fat: 10g; Saturated Fat: 1g; Protein: 6g; Carbohydrates: 0.5g; Sodium: 116mg; Fiber: 3g; Sugar: 1g

Ingredients

2.5 cups almond flour

8 oz. cream cheese, full-fat

1.5 tsp baking powder, gluten-free

0.25 cup coconut flour

0.5 cup butter, unsalted

1 tsp rosemary seasoning

8 whole eggs

1 tsp sage seasoning

2 tbsp parsley seasoning

3 tsp butter, unsalted and separate

Directions

Heat the stove at a temperature of 350°F.

Prepare a 8 x 4-inch bread loaf pan thoroughly with one tbsp. of butter and set to the side.

Blend the cream cheese and the leftover ½ cup of butter in a food blender for approximately 45 seconds until the consistency is smooth.

Combine the parsley, sage, and rosemary into the blender and pulse for another half minute until integrated.

Whip one egg in the blender until combined. Repeat for the other 7 eggs until complete.

Finally, blend the coconut flour, baking powder, and almond flour for an additional 90 seconds until the batter is a thick consistency.

Distribute to the prepped pan evenly while smoothing with a scraper.

Utilize a utensil to see if any residue remains after poking into the center.

Transfer to the countertop and wait approximately 15 minutes before dividing and serving.

Muffins

Keto blueberry muffins

Prep 10 minutes/ Cook 25 minutes / Serves 12/ 360°F

Difficulty: Beginner

PER SERVING: Calories: 124; Carbohydrates: 5g; Fat: 7g; saturated fat: 2g; Sodium: 154mg; Fiber: 2g; Protein: 3g

Ingredients

1/3 cups keto friendly sugar

1 ½ tsps. baking powder

½ tsp baking soda

½ cups almond flour

½ tsp kosher salt

1/3 cups butter, melted

1/3 cups almond milk

3 Large eggs

1 tsp pure vanilla extract

2/3 cups fresh blueberries

Directions

Preheat the oven to 360ºF.

Line your Pan size: 15.75"x 11.25" muffin pan with cupcake liners or grease it.

Add almond flour, sugar, baking powder, baking soda, and salt to a bowl then whisk to combine

Add your wet ingredients, that is, the melted butter, almond milk, eggs and vanilla extract to another bowl then mix.

Add butter mixture to the mixture of dry ingredients then stir to mix.

Gently fold in your blueberries.

Scoop batter onto the muffin pan to a level of about ¾.

Bake for about 25 minutes.

Insert a toothpick into a muffin. If the muffins are ready, it should come out clean.

Allow to cool for 5-10 minutes.

Keto chocolate chip muffins

Prep 10/ Cook 20/ Serves 6/ 350°F

Difficulty: Intermediate

PER SERVING: Calories: 229; Fat: 12g; Saturated Fat: 2g; Protein: 7g; Carbohydrates: 11g; Sodium: 96mg; Fiber: 0g; Sugar: 2g

Ingredients

1 Cup Almond Flour

2 large eggs

1 tsp baking powder

¼ cup Erythritol

40g Butter (melted)

40 ml unsweetened almond milk

1 tsp Vanilla Extract

50g (Unsweetened) Dark Chocolate

Directions

Preheat your oven to a temperature of 350°F.

Line your 13.75"x 10.5" muffin pan with cupcake liners or grease it.

Mix the almond flour and the baking powder together in a bowl.

Add 2 eggs into the bowl and stir to mix.

Melt the butter then add into the bowl.

Add the other ingredients (apart from the chocolate) and whisk.

Spoon the batter into your muffin tray filling it up to a level of ¾.

Cut the pieces of chocolate into thin slices.

Pierce them through the top of the muffins.

Bake for 20 minutes. A toothpick should come out clean when poked through the muffin.

Let them cool for 5-10 minutes.

Keto coffee cake muffins

Prep 20 minutes/ Cook 25 minutes/ Serves 12/ 3555°F

Difficulty: Intermediate

PER SERVING: Calories: 222; Total Fat: 18g; Cholesterol: 72mg; Sodium:156mg; Protein: 7g; Potassium: 73mg; Carbohydrates: 9g

Ingredients

2 tbsps. butter softened

2 ounces cream cheese softened

1 tsp baking powder

¼ cup tsp salt

1/3 cup Swerve

2 tsp vanilla

½ cup unsweetened almond milk

1 cup almond flour

½ cup coconut flour

4 eggs

(Topping)

1 tsp cinnamon

2 tbsps coconut flour

¼ cup Swerve

¼ cup butter softened

1 cup almond flour

Ingredients

Preheat oven to 355ºF. Line a muffin tin with paper liners or grease the muffin tin.

Place cream cheese, vanilla and eggs in a food processor and blend until well combined.

Put the dry ingredients to a big bowl and thoroughly mix.

Combine the dry and wet ingredients and whisk.

For the topping add your ingredients together in a separate bowl and mix.

Bake 25 minutes until golden. When you insert toothpick, it should come out clean.

Keto pumpkin muffins

Prep 10 minutes/ Cook 20 minutes/ Serves 16/ 350°F

Difficulty: Beginner

PER SERVING: Calories: 121; Carbohydrates:3g; Protein: 2g; Fat: 10g; Cholesterol: 55mg; Sodium: 116mg; Potassium: 95mg; Fiber: 1g

Ingredients

5 eggs

½ cup liquid coconut oil

2 tbsp butter

1 cup pumpkin puree

1 ½ tbsp. pumpkin pie spice

1 ½ cup Swerve

2 tsps. vanilla extract

½ cup coconut flour

1 tsp salt

1 ½ tsps. baking powder

Filling

2 ounces cream cheese

2 tbsps heavy whipping cream

1 tbsps swerve or sweetener of your choice

1 tsp vanilla extract

Directions

Preheat oven to 350ºF then grease the 15.75" x 11.25"muffin pan or line it with muffin liners.

Melt the butter.

Add eggs, coconut oil, melted butter, pumpkin puree, pumpkin pie spice, swerve and vanilla extract to a large bowl and mix until well combined.

Add coconut flour, salt and baking powder to the other ingredients and mix.

Scoop batter into prepared muffin tins, filling each one 3/4 way.

In another bowl, add the ingredients for the filling and stir until well combined and smooth.

Place 1 tsp of filling in the center of each muffin.

Using a toothpick swirl cream cheese batter into muffin

Bake for 20 minutes.

Notes: these muffins need a thicker batter than most muffins do.

Prep 10 minutes/ Cook 25 minutes/ Serves 6/ 350°F

Difficulty: Beginner

PER SERVING: Calories: 184; Carbohydrates:4g; Protein: 7g; Fat: 14g; Cholesterol: 23mg; Sodium: 43mg; Potassium: 95mg; Fiber: 1g; Sugar: 1g

Ingredients

0.125 cup Erythritol sweetener, confectioner

0.75 cup almond flour

1.25 tbsp ground flax

3 tbsp butter, unsalted and melted

0.125 cup sour cream, full-fat

1.25 tsp baking powder, gluten-free

4 oz. walnuts, raw and chopped

0.33 tsp ground cinnamon

2 tsp butter, unsalted, cubed and separate

1.5 tsp banana extract, sugar-free

2 tsp almond flour, separate

0.125 cup almond milk, unsweetened

1 tsp vanilla extract, sugar-free

2 tsp Erythritol sweetener, confectioner and separate

1 large egg

Directions

Dissolve the 3 tsp. of butter completely in a 6.5" saucepan and set to the side.

Adjust the temperature of the stove to heat at 350°F. Line a small cupcake tin with 6 papers or silicone cups. Set aside.

Use a food blender to pulse the 2 tsp. of almond flour, 2 tsp. of butter and walnuts until a crumbly consistency. Set to the side.

Blend the 1/3 cup of Erythritol, cinnamon, baking powder and ¾ cup of almond flour until incorporated fully.

Combine the eggs, sour cream, banana extract, almond milk, melted butter, and vanilla extract into the mixture until integrated.

Evenly distribute to the prepped cupcake tin and dust with the crumble from the food processor. Apply slight pressure to adhere to the batter.

Evenly spread the 2 tsp. of Erythritol over the muffins.

Heat for a total of 20 minutes and take out of the stove to the countertop.

Wait about half an hour before serving. Enjoy!

Cinnamon Muffins

Prep 11 minutes / Cook 20 minutes / Serves 12/ 350°F

Difficulty: Beginner

PER SERVING: Calories: 89; Fat: 9g; Saturated Fat: 2g; Protein: 5g; Carbohydrates: 1.8g; Sodium: 132mg; Fiber: 0g; Sugar: 2g

Ingredients

For the muffin:

0.33 cup almond flour

0.5 tsp baking powder, gluten-free

0.33 cup almond butter

0.5 tbsp ground cinnamon

5 oz. pumpkin puree

0.33 cup coconut oil

12 cavity muffin tin or 24 cavity mini muffin tin

For the optional topping:

0.125 cup coconut butter

0.5 tbsp. Swerve sweetener, granulated

0.125 cup milk

1.25 tsp. lemon juice

Directions

Set your stove to heat at the temperature of 350°F.

Use silicone or baking cups to line your preferred cupcake tin. Set to the side.

Combine the almond flour, baking powder, and cinnamon with a whisk in a glass dish. Remove any lumpiness present.

Blend the almond butter, pumpkin puree, and coconut oil into the mix until incorporated.

Evenly divide the batter between the cavities in the prepped cupcake tin.

Heat for approximately 13 minutes and transfer to a wire rack after waiting 5 minutes.

If you are applying the topping, blend the lemon juice, milk, Swerve, and coconut butter until smooth.

Evenly empty the topping once the muffins have completely cooled.

Prep 15 minutes / Cook 30 minutes / Serves 12/ 350ºF

Difficulty: Beginner

PER SERVING: Calories: 189; Protein: 7g; Net carbohydrates: 3.5g; Fat: 16g; Sugar: 1g

Ingredients

0.5 tsp salt

2 cups almond flour, blanched

0.5 cup cocoa powder, unsweetened

0.75 cup Pyure Stevia blend, granulated

1 tsp. baking powder, gluten-free

4 large eggs

0.25 cup coconut oil, melted

2 oz. almond milk, unsweetened

1 tsp vanilla extract, sugar-free

1.75 oz. dark chocolate, Stevia sweetened and chopped

Directions

Set the temperature of the stove to heat at 350°F. Cover the cavities of the cupcake tin with baking liner or silicone. Set to the side.

Liquefy the coconut oil for approximately 3 minutes in a saucepan.

Chop the chocolate roughly into small chunks and set aside.

Blend the salt, baking powder, almond flour, Pyure Stevia blend, and cocoa powder until fully incorporated.

Combine the melted coconut oil, vanilla extract, almond milk, and eggs into the mix and toss until integrated.

Finally, incorporate the chopped chocolate into the mix.

Evenly divide the batter to the prepped cupcake tin.

For the duration of approximately 26 minutes, heat the muffins and then transfer to the countertop.

Wait about 10 minutes before serving and enjoy!

Prep 10 minutes/ Cook 30 minutes/ Serves 12/ 325°F

Difficulty: Intermediate

PER SERVING: Calories: 284; Protein: 9g; Net carbohydrates: 3.9g; Fat: 24g; Sugar: 1g

Ingredients

For the muffins:

0.5 tsp ground cinnamon

2 cups almond flour

0.5 cup almond milk, unsweetened

0.33 cup Swerve sweetener, granulated

3 tbsp coconut flour

0.25 tsp. salt

3 tsp baking powder, gluten-free

0.5 cup butter, unsalted

4 large eggs

0.5 tsp vanilla extract, sugar-free

12 cavity muffin tin

For the optional topping:

0.5 cup almond flour

3 tbsp. Sukrin Gold brown sugar substitute

0.25 cup butter, unsalted and melted

2 tbsp. coconut flour

0.75 tsp. ground cinnamon

Directions

Adjust your stove to heat at the temperature of 325°F.

Cover the 12 cavities with silicone or baking cups and set to the side.

Blend the salt, cinnamon, baking powder, coconut flour, Swerve, and almond flour in a glass dish until all lumpiness is no longer present.

Combine the vanilla extract, almond milk, eggs, and butter into the mix and blend until incorporated fully.

Equally distribute to the prepped cupcake tin.

For the optional glaze, dissolve the butter in a saucepan and turn the burner off.

Combine the cinnamon, coconut flour, Sukrin Gold, and almond flour in a 2.125" round pan and evenly distribute to the top of the batter.

Heat in the stove for approximately half an hour and take out to place on the countertop.

Wait about 10 minutes before serving and enjoy!

Prep 10 minutes / Cook 30 minutes/ Serves 12/ 350ºF

Difficulty: Expert

PER SERVING: Calories: 130; Protein: 4g; Net carbohydrates: 1.7g; Fat: 12g; Sugar: 0g

Ingredients

0.25 cup golden flaxseed meal

0.75 cup almond flour

0.33 cup Erythritol sweetener, granulated

2 tbsp poppy seeds

1 tbsp baking powder, gluten-free

3 large eggs

0.25 cup butter, salted and melted

2 tbsp lemon zest

0.25 cup heavy cream

25 drops Stevia liquid

1 tsp vanilla extract, sugar-free

3 tbsp lemon juice

Directions

Liquefy the butter in a 5.5" saucepan and turn the burner off.

In the meantime, prepare a muffin tin with baking cups or silicone. Set to the side.

Heat your stove to the temperature of 350°F.

Combine the poppy seeds, Erythritol, flaxseed meal, and almond flour with a whisk until integrated.

Blend the heavy cream, eggs, and melted butter until incorporated fully.

Finally combine the lemon juice, vanilla extract, Stevia liquid, baking powder, and lemon zest into the mix and blend well.

Divide the batter equally to the prepped muffin tin and heat for approximately 20 minutes.

Place on the countertop and wait about 10 minutes before serving.

Buns

Keto hamburger buns

Prep 5 minutes / Cook 15 minutes / Serves 5/ 400ºF

Difficulty: Expert

PER SERVING: Calories: 294; Carbohydrates: 7g; Protein:14g; Fat: 25g; Fiber: 3g

Ingredients

1 ¼ cup almond flour

1 ½ cup mozzarella cheese (part skim grated)

2 oz cream cheese

1 egg (large)

2 tbsps oat fiber 500/ protein powder

1 tbsp baking powder

Directions

Using a microwave safe bowl, put the cream cheese and mozzarella cheese. Microwave the cheese for I minutes. Remove the bowl, stir and microwave again for 40 seconds to another minute.

Scrape out the cheese and place it together with the egg into a food processor. Stop when it's smooth. Add your dry ingredients, processing it till dough is formed. (It is normally very sticky) Let the dough cool.

Preheat your oven to 400°F, placing the rack in the middle. Line your baking sheet with parchment paper and place the cheap metal plate or pan at the bottom of the oven.

Once the oven is ready, separate the dough into 5 equal portions. Apply oil on your hands (not too much) and roll the portions into balls. Place them on the parchment paper, flattening them a bit while creating a domed shape.

Put 5 or 6 ice cubes on the metal pan and place the buns inside the oven. The steam from the cubes will make the buns rise.

Bake them for about fifteen minutes. They should be done once they brown on the outside. If not, give them more minutes in the oven.

Note: Store in the fridge in an airtight container.

Paleo, Keto buns

Prep 10 minutes / Cook 45 minutes / Serves 10/ 350ºF

Difficulty: Beginner

PER SERVING: Calories: 169; Iron: 0.7mg; Calcium: 45mg; Fiber: 4g; Potassium: 50mg; Sodium: 38mg; Cholesterol: 14mg; Saturated fat: 4g; Fat

Ingredients

1 ½ cup (150g) almond meal

½ cup (60g) coconut flour

½ cup flax meal

2/3 cup psyllium husks

6 egg whites (large)

2 eggs (large)

5 tbsps sesame seeds

2 tsps. garlic powder

2 tsps. cream of tartar/ apple cider vinegar

2 tsp onion powder

1 tsp baking soda

1 tsp sea salt/ pink Himalayan

2 tbsps Erythritol (optional)

480 ml boiling water

Directions

Preheat your oven to 350°F

Mix all your dry ingredients in a mixing bowl.

Add your egg whites and eggs. Use a hand mixer to process it till your dough becomes thick.

Add the boiling water and process until it combines.

Line your baking sheet with parchment paper.

Use a spoon to make the buns and create a dome shape.

Sprinkle the sesame seeds on the buns. Press the seeds into the buns to prevent them from falling out.

Bake for 45 minutes.

Almond Buns

Prep 10 minutes / Cook 17 minutes / Serves 3/ 350° F

Difficulty: Intermediate

PER SERVING: Calories: 373, Fat: 35 g, Protein: 10 g, Carbohydrates: 4g, Sodium: 423mg; Fiber: 2g; Sugar: 1g

Ingredients:

¾ cup almond flour

1 ½ tsps. baking powder

2 eggs, large & preferably farm-raised

1 ½ tsp Splenda

5 tbsps butter, organic & melted

Ingredients:

To make almond buns, combine almond flour, Splenda, baking powder in a large mixing bowl.

To this, add the eggs one at a time and whisk them well.

Next, spoon in the melted butter and whisk until everything comes together.

Divide the mixture into six portions and place them on a muffin top 13.75"x 10.25" pan. Spread it evenly.

Finally, bake at 350° F for 13 to 17 minutes or until the edges start to brown. Tip: keep a close watch.

Allow it to cool completely before serving.

Sesame Buns

Prep 10 minutes / Cook 45 minutes / Serves 6/ 350ºF

Difficulty: Beginner

PER SERVING: Calories: 135; Iron: 22mg; Calcium: 32mg; Fiber: 4g; Sodium: 54mg; Cholesterol: 23mg; Saturated fat: 2g; Fat Time: 25 minutes

Ingredients:

1 tsp kosher or sea salt

2 tsp baking powder

4 tbsp butter (melted)

2 cups mozzarella cheese (shredded)

3 cups almond meal or almond flour

3 big eggs

4 ounces cream cheese

dried parsley

sesame seeds

Directions:

First, preheat your oven to 400°F and use paper liners to line your muffin tin.

In a microwave-safe container, combine the cream cheese and mozzarella cheese. Place the container in the microwave and melt at intervals of 30-seconds each.

Add the eggs then stir to incorporate. Add the salt, almond meal (or flour), and baking powder then continue stirring to combine.

Form the dough into balls, place on your baking sheet, and press down slightly to flatten

Brush the top of each bun with melted butter and top with parsley and sesame seeds.

Place the baking sheet in the oven and bake the sesame buns for 10 to 12 minutes.

Prep 10 minutes/ Cook 20 minutes / Serves 4/ 380°F

Difficulty: Intermediate

PER SERVING: Calories- 218; Fat- 13.5g, Carbs- 7.2g, Dietary fiber- 3.5g, Protein- 17g.

Ingredients

½ cup coconut flour

1 ½ cups mozzarella cheese (shredded)

2 tbsps cream cheese (softened)

2 tbsps flax meal

2 eggs (large)

1 tbsp baking powder

1 tbsp sesame seeds

½ tsp salt

Directions

Preheat your oven to 380°F.

Using a mixing bowl, whisk your flax meal, coconut flour, salt and baking soda.

In another bowl, put your cream cheese and mozzarella cheese. Microwave your cheese for 45 seconds to a minute. Stir it and microwave once more until it becomes melted.

Beat your eggs, adding into the first bowl which has the dry ingredients. Add the cheese too to the bowl. You can use your hand mixer to make the dough.

Separate the dough into four equal portions. Use these portions to make the buns and sprinkle sesame seeds. Press the seeds to prevent them from falling out.

Line the baking sheet with parchment paper and place your buns.

Bake for 20 minutes or until they brown on the outside.

Leave them to cool.

Cookies

Low-Carb Chocolate Chip Cookies

Prep 10 minutes/ Cook 12 minutes / Serves 12/ 350ºF

Difficulty: Intermediate

PER SERVING: Calories 148, Fat: 14 g, Protein: 3 g, Carbs: 3 g,

Ingredients

1.5 cups Almond Flour

½ tsp Baking Powder

¼ tsp Salt

1 cup Sugar-Free Chocolate Chips

1 stick Butter, softened

1 tsp Vanilla Extract

½ cup Swerve Granular Sweetener

1 Whole Egg

Directions

Preheat oven to 350°F.

Cream butter and sweetener with a mixer.

Mix in the egg and vanilla extract.

Whisk together the almond flour, baking powder, and salt in a separate bowl.

Mix the dry ingredients into the wet mixture.

Fold in the chocolate chips into the dough.

Scoop the dough into a baking sheet lined with parchment. Press slightly to flatten.

Bake for 12 minutes.

Apricot and Cream Cheese Cookies

Prep 10 minutes/ Cook 12 minutes / Serves 15/ 350ºF

Difficulty: Beginner-Intermediate-Expert

PER SERVING: Calories: 122, Fat: 11 g, Protein: 4 g, Carbohydrates: 3 g, Fiber 0.9g

Ingredients:

2 cups Almond Flour

½ tsp Baking Powder

¼ tsp Salt

¼ cup Cream Cheese, softened

¼ cup Sugar-Free Apricot Preserve

¼ cup Butter, softened

1 tsp Vanilla Extract

½ cup Swerve Granular Sweetener

1 Whole Egg

Directions

Preheat oven to 350°F

With a hand mixer, beat together the butter, cream cheese, sweetener, and apricot preserve until fluffy.

Mix in the egg and vanilla extract.

Whisk together the almond flour, baking powder, and salt in a separate bowl.

Mix the dry ingredients into the wet mixture.

Scoop the dough into a baking sheet lined with parchment. Press slightly to flatten.

Bake for 12 minutes.

Almond Butter Cookies

Prep 10 minutes/ Cook 12 minutes / Serves 12/ 350°F

Difficulty: Intermediate

PER SERVING: Calories: 159, Fat: 14 g, Protein: 5 g, Carbs: 5 g

Ingredients:

1 cup Almond Butter

¼ cup Coconut Flour

½ cup Erythritol

¼ cup Slivered Almonds

1 Whole Egg

1 tsp Vanilla Extract

Directions

Preheat oven to 350°F.

Mix together the almond butter, coconut flour, erythritol, vanilla, and egg in a bowl until well combined.

Fold in the slivered almonds.

Scoop the dough into a baking sheet lined with parchment. Press slightly to flatten.

Bake for 12 minutes.

Choco Hazelnut Butter Cookies

Prep 10 minutes/ Cook 12 minutes / Serves 12/ 350ºF

Difficulty: Intermediate

PER SERVING: Calories: 168, Fat: 8 g, Protein: 1 g, Protein: 7g; Carbohydrates: 2g; Sodium: 96mg; Fiber: 0g; Sugar: 1g

Ingredients

1 cup Hazelnut Butter

¼ cup Unsweetened Cocoa Powder

½ cup Erythritol

¼ cup Sugar-Free Chocolate Chips

1 Whole Egg

¼ cup Almond Milk

1 tsp Vanilla Extract

Directions

Preheat oven to 350°F.

Mix together the hazelnut butter, cocoa powder, and erythritol in a bowl until well combined.

Stir in the egg and vanilla extract.

Add in milk a tbsp at a time.

Fold in the chocolate chips.

Scoop the dough into a baking sheet lined with parchment. Press slightly to flatten.

Bake for 12 minutes.

Banana Walnut Cookies

Prep 10 minutes/ Cook 12 minutes / Serves 12/ 350ºF

Difficulty: Beginner

PER SERVING: Calories: 112, Fat: 8 g, Saturated Fat: 1g; Protein: 3 g, Carbohydrates: 8 g; Fiber: 1g; Sugar: 1g

Ingredients

1.5 cups Almond Flour

1 cup Mashed Bananas

¼ cup Peanut Butter

¼ cup Walnuts, chopped

Directions

Preheat oven to 350°F.

In a bowl, mix almond flour, mashed bananas, and peanut butter until well combined.

Fold in the walnuts into the dough.

Scoop the dough into a baking sheet lined with parchment. Press slightly to flatten.

Bake for 12 minutes.

Pancakes

Almond Banana Pancakes

Prep 10 minutes/ Cook 10 minutes / Serves 4

Difficulty: Beginner

PER SERVING: Calories: 235, Fat: 17 g, Saturated Fat: 3g
Carbohydrates: 10 g, Protein: 11 g, Sodium: 116mg; Fiber: 3g;
Sugar: 1g

Ingredients

1 Ripe Banana, mashed

4 Eggs

½ cup Almond Flour

2 tbsp Erythritol

1 tsp Baking Powder

1 tsp Ground Cinnamon

Directions

Whisk together almond flour, baking powder, and cinnamon in a bowl.

In a separate bowl, mix together mashed banana, eggs, and erythritol.

Gradually fold in the dry ingredients into the wet mixture.

Preheat a skillet and coat with non-stick spray.

Ladle in the batter and cook for 1-2 minutes per side.

Prep 5 minutes/ Cook 10 minutes/ Serves 4

Difficulty: Intermediate

PER SERVING: Calories: 230, Fat: 19 g, Saturated Fat: 3g; Protein: 10 g, Carbs: 2 g, Fiber: 3g; Sugar: 1g

Ingredients

½ cup Cream Cheese

4 Eggs

½ cup Almond Flour

1 tbsp Minced Jalapenos

Directions

Mix all ingredients in a blender.

Preheat a skillet and coat with non-stick spray.

Ladle in the batter and cook for 1-2 minutes per side.

Prep 5 minutes/ Cook 10 minutes/ Serves 4

Difficulty: Beginner

PER SERVING: Calories: 333,   Fat: 30 g, Protein: 10 g, Carbohydrates: 6 g, Sodium: 106mg; Fiber: 1g; Sugar: 2g

Ingredients

½ cup Coconut Flour

4 Eggs

1 cup Coconut Milk

1 tsp Psyllium Husk

½ tsp Baking Powder

1 tbsp Coconut Oil

1 tbsp Chia Seeds

Directions

Mix all ingredients in a blender.

Preheat a skillet and coat with non-stick spray.

Ladle in the batter and cook for 1-2 minutes per side.

Keto Blueberry Pancakes

Prep 10 minutes/ Cook 10 minutes/ Serves 4

Difficulty: Beginner

PER SERVING: Calories: 287, Fat: 25 g, Saturated Fat: 5g; Protein: 11 g, Carbohydrates: 4 g; Fiber: 0g; Sugar: 3g

Ingredients

½ cup Cream Cheese

4 Eggs

2 tbsp Melted Butter

½ cup Almond Flour

2 tbsp Erythritol

1 tsp Baking Powder

¼ tsp Salt

¼ cup Fresh Blueberries

Directions

Whisk together almond flour, baking powder, and salt in a bowl.

In a separate bowl, mix together cream cheese, eggs, butter, and erythritol.

Gradually stir in the dry ingredients into the wet mixture.

Fold in the blueberries.

Preheat a skillet and coat with non-stick spray.

Ladle in the batter and cook for 1-2 minutes per side.

Spiced Pumpkin Pancakes

Prep 10 minutes/ Cook 10 minutes/ Serves 4

Difficulty: Intermediate

PER SERVING: Calories: 280, Fat: 23 g, Saturated Fat: 5g; Protein: 12 g, Carbs: 9 g, Fiber: 3g; Sugar: 2g

Ingredients

1 cup Almond Flour

1 tbsp Pumpkin Pie Spice

½ tsp Baking Powder

2 tbsp Erythritol

3 Eggs

¼ cup Pumpkin Puree

¼ cup Coconut Milk

Directions

Mix all ingredients in a blender.

Preheat a skillet and coat with non-stick spray.

Ladle in the batter and cook for 1-2 minutes per side.

Prep 5 minutes/ Cook 10 minutes/ Serves 4

Difficulty: Expert

PER SERVING: Calories: 339, Fat: 29 g, Saturated Fat: 9g; Protein: 13 g, Carbohydrates: 5 g, Fiber: 1g; Sugar: 2g

Ingredients

½ cup Cream Cheese

4 Eggs

2 tbsp Butter, melted

½ cup Almond Flour

1 tbsp Unsweetened Cocoa Powder

2 tbsp Erythritol

1 tsp Vanilla Extract

½ tsp Red Food Coloring

Directions

Mix all ingredients in a blender.

Preheat a skillet and coat with non-stick spray.

Ladle in the batter and cook for 1-2 minutes per side.

Prep 5 minutes/ Cook 10/ minutes Serves 4

Difficulty: Intermediate

PER SERVING: Calories:256, Fat: 20 g, Saturated Fat: 1g; Protein: 15 g, Carbohydrates: 5 g, Fiber: 1g; Sugar: 1g

Ingredients

½ cup Ricotta Cheese

4 Eggs

½ cup Almond Flour

1 tsp Orange Zest

1 tsp Vanilla Extract

Directions

Mix all ingredients in a blender.

Preheat a skillet and coat with non-stick spray.

Ladle in the batter and cook for 1-2 minutes per side.

Prep 10 minutes / Cook 10 minutes / Serves 4

Difficulty: Intermediate

PER SERVING: Calories: 290, Fat: 22 g, Protein: 17 g, Carbohydrates: 6 g, Sodium: 79mg; Fiber: 2g; Sugar: 3g

Ingredients

½ cup Shredded Cheddar

4 Eggs, separated

½ cup Almond Flour

½ tsp Cream of Tartar

¼ tsp Salt

¼ cup Bacon Bits

1 tbsp Chopped Chives

Directions

Whisk the egg whites and cream of tartar until soft peaks from.

Sift in the almond flour and salt.

Fold in the cheddar, bacon, and chives.

Lightly coat a 10" non-stick pan with cooking spray.

Ladle the batter in and cook for 1-2 minutes per side.

Croissants

French Croissant

Prep 40 minutes / Cook 15 minutes / Serves 12

Difficulty: Expert

PER SERVING: Calories: 196, Fat: 22 g, Protein: 13.4 g, Carbohydrates: 6 g, Sodium: 304mg; Fiber: 0.6g; Sugar: 2g

Ingredients:

1.75 cups all-purpose flour

0.75 cup milk, warm

1 tsp white sugar

2 tsp white sugar

1.5 tsp salt

¾ cup chilled unsalted butter

3 tbsp warm water

2 tbsp vegetable oil

1.5 tsp dry yeast

1 tbsp water

1 egg

Directions:

Mix water, yeast and 1 tsp sugar and set aside until it becomes creamy.

Add flour to a mixing bowl and add milk salt and sugar. Combine with the yeast mixture and thoroughly mix. Set aside for about 3 hours to let it rise.

Apply butter till it is pliable. Pat the dough on a rectangle which is 14"x8" and smear butter on 2/3 and leave a 1/3 margin. Fold the 1/3 which is not buttered over the third at the center and the 1/3 top third which is buttered over that. Turn right and roll it on the triangle and fold thrice. Drizzle some flour and put in plastic bag

Roll dough on the rectangle and cut crosswise into two. Shape one of the two while the other is chilling. Cut into squares of 5x5" and half diagonally cut the squares and elongate every triangle by rolling.

Put on a baking sheet and let them rise.

Mix egg, water in a different bowl and glaze the croissant. Bake for 15 minutes. Cool before serving.

Pumpkin Pie Baked Croissants

Prep 10 minutes / Cook 20 minutes / Serves 6

Difficulty: Expert

PER SERVING: Calories: 110, Fat: 10 g, Protein: 10 g, Carbohydrates: 6g, Sodium: 244mg; Fiber: 0.6g; Sugar: 2g

Ingredients:

1 cup unsalted butter (at room temperature)

½ cup granulated sugar

1 cup pureed pumpkin

1 egg

1 tbsp. all-purpose flour

2 tsp vanilla essence

2 tsp pumpkin pie spice

Pinch kosher salt

6 large bakery croissants (halved lengthwise)

Confectioner's sugar (for dusting)

Directions:

Preheat the main oven to 350°F. Line a baking sheet with parchment.

Beat together the butter and granulated sugar until fluffy.

Beat in the pureed pumpkin, egg, all-purpose flour, vanilla essence, pie spice, and kosher salt for 2-3 minutes until super light.

Spread 1-2 tbsp. of the mixture into each sliced croissant.

Arrange the filled croissants on a baking sheet. Spread any remaining pumpkin mixture on top of the croissants.

Place in the oven and bake for 20 minutes.

Allow to cool a little before dusting with confectioner's sugar and serving warm.

Prep 20 minutes / Cook 25 minutes / Serves 8/ 450°F

Difficulty: Expert

PER SERVING: Calories: 290, Fat: 22 g, Protein: 5.5g, Carbohydrates: 5g, Sodium: 267mg; Fiber: 1.5g; Sugar: 5.4g

Ingredients:

2 cups flour

1 tbsp milk

½ tsp salt

½ cup warm milk

25g fresh yeast

1 egg yolk

3 tbsp sugar

Egg Wash

1.25 sticks unsalted butter, diced

Directions

Put fresh yeast in a bowl. Stir in sugar until it dissolves. Pour in the milk and let it cool.

In a bowl, mix salt and flour and then add butter. Combine using a fork to form crumbles.

Pour in the yeast mixture and mix to form dough. Wrap the butter in a plastic so as to keep it in pea-size pieces and put in a freezer for half an hour.

Dust the rolling pin and the working surface and the roll the dough into rectangular shape.

Fold the widths of the dough to the center. Twist the dough for a ¼ turn and roll it and fold the edges.

Turn the dough upside down and repeat the folding.

Cover the dough in a plastic and put in the refrigerator for a few hours.

Roll dough on a surface drizzled with flour into a four-sided shape (rectangle). Cut the dough using a knife into triangles.

Make a slit on each triangle's center and stretch the tip and corners roll then to form a croissant.

Put the croissants on the parchment paper-lined baking sheet and cover and allow 2 hours to rise.

Preheat oven to 450°F. use the egg wash to brush the croissants.

Bake for 10 minutes and lower the temperature to 375°F and bake for 15 more minutes. Put on a rack to cool and serve.

Prep 10 minutes / Cook 5 minutes / Serves 6

Difficulty: Intermediate

PER SERVING: Calories: 211, Fat: 13 g, Protein: 9 g, Carbohydrates: 5.6 g, Sodium: 342mg; Fiber: 2g; Sugar: 4g

Ingredients:

2 tsp brown sugar

2 tsp cinnamon

2 tsp nutmeg

4 tbsp. salted butter (melted)

6 large croissants (halved lengthwise)

18 large marshmallows

6 ounces semisweet chocolate squares

Directions:

Preheat your grill for direct grilling on a moderately high heat.

Combine the sugar, cinnamon, and nutmeg in a small dish.

Brush each croissant half with melted butter on the cut-sides only. Sprinkle each croissant half with the spiced sugar.

Take 6 skewers and slide 3 marshmallows onto each.

Toast each croissant half, buttered side down, for 60 seconds. Take off the grill and divide the chocolate squares equally among the bottom halves.

Grill the marshmallows for 90 seconds, turning once. Slide 3 marshmallows onto each chocolatey croissant base.

Sandwich together with the toasted croissant tops.

Enjoy straight away!

Prep 10 minutes/ Cook 45 minutes / Serves 6

Difficulty: Expert

PER SERVING: Calories: 135, Fat: 11 g, Saturated Fat: 2g Carbohydrates: 5 g, Protein: 10 g, Sodium: 201mg; Fiber: 2g; Sugar: 2g

Ingredients:

2 medium eggs

cup granulated sugar

2 cups whole milk

tsp kosher salt

4 large croissants (torn into pieces)

3 tbsp. flaked almonds

Butter (for greasing)

Directions:

Preheat the main oven to 300 degrees F. Grease a (1½-2 quart) shallow baking dish.

Whisk together the eggs, granulated sugar, whole milk, and kosher salt until well combined.

Toss the torn croissants in the liquid until coated. Set aside to soak for 7-9 minutes.

Transfer the mixture to the baking dish and use a spatula to smooth down the surface. Scatter with the flaked almonds.

Place in the oven and bake for approximately 45 minutes, until the custard has set.

Allow to stand for several minutes before slicing and serving.

Pizza

Cauliflower Pizza Crust

Prep 10 minutes/ Cook 35 minutes/ Serves 8/ 405°F

Difficulty: Expert

PER SERVING: Calories: 278; Fat: 21g; Saturated Fat: 2g; Protein: 11g; Carbohydrates: 5g; Sodium: 102mg; Fiber: 1g; Sugar: 3g

Ingredients

0.5 tsp salt

16 oz. cauliflower florets

1 large egg

1.5 tbsp coconut flour

3 tsp avocado oil

0.5 tsp Italian seasoning

1 tsp coconut oil

Directions

Set your oven to heat at the temperature of 405°F.

Pulse the cauliflower in a food blender for approximately 60 seconds until it is a crumbly consistency.

Heat the coconut oil and cauliflower in a 9"x 9" frypan for approximately 5 minutes as it becomes tender.

Transfer the cauliflower to a kitchen towel and twist to eliminate the extra water. Repeat this step as many times as necessary to make sure the moisture has been eliminated.

Prepare your 10" pizza pan or flat sheet with a section of baking lining and set to the side.

In a glass dish, blend the riced cauliflower, salt, egg, coconut flour, avocado oil, and Italian seasoning and integrate until it thickens.

Flatten the dough onto the prepped pan to no less than a quarter inch.

Heat for 25 minutes if then and up to half an hour if thicker.

Complete with your favorite toppings and finish in the stove for another 5 minutes. Enjoy!

Prep 7 minutes/ Cook 25 minutes/ Serves 8/ 350°F

Difficulty: Intermediate

PER SERVING: Calories: 190, Carbohydrates: 1.4 g, Fat: 6 g, Saturated Fat: 1g; Fiber: 2g Sugar: 2g

Ingredients

1.5 cups mozzarella cheese, shredded

0.75 cup almond flour

1 whole egg

2 tbsp cream cheese, full-fat

0.25 tsp salt

Directions

Set your stove to heat at the temperature of 350°F.

Use a microwave-safe dish to nuke the almond flour, mozzarella, and cream cheese for approximately 60 seconds until liquefied.

Toss the cheese and heat for an additional half minute.

Blend the salt and egg into the cheese for about half a minute.

Place a section of baking lining on the counter and transfer the dough to the middle. Use another section of baking lining to place on top.

Flatten to no less than a quarter of an inch. Separate the top baking lining and transfer to 10" pan.

Heat for approximately 13 minutes until turning golden.

Layer with your toppings of choice and heat for about 5 minutes.

Serve hot and enjoy!

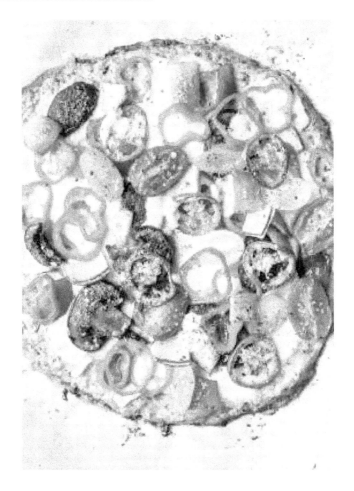

Prep 15 minutes/ Cook 45minutes/ Serves 8/ 400°F

Difficulty: Intermediate

PER SERVING: Calories: 127, Protein: 7g, Fat: 8 g, Saturated Fat: 2g; Carbohydrates: 4 g, Fiber: 1g; Sugar: 2g

Ingredients

4 cups zucchini, shredded

1 cup almond flour

2.75 tbsp coconut flour

4 tbsp nutritional yeast

1.33 tbsp Italian seasoning

0.75 tsp salt

3 large eggs

Directions

Adjust the temperature of your stove to heat at 400°F.

Cover a 12.75" pan with a layer of baking lining and set to the side.

Use a kitchen grater to shred the zucchini using the largest holes available.

Transfer to a kitchen towel and wring to release all excess moisture.

In a glass dish, blend the coconut flour, zucchini, salt, Italian seasoning, nutritional yeast, eggs, and almond flour until integrated and thickened.

Distribute to the prepped sheet and flatten to no less than quarter an inch by hand.

Heat for the duration of 20 minutes. Turn the crust over and warm for another 10 minutes.

Layer with your preferred toppings and heat for another 13 minutes.

Wait about 10 minutes before slicing and serving. Enjoy!

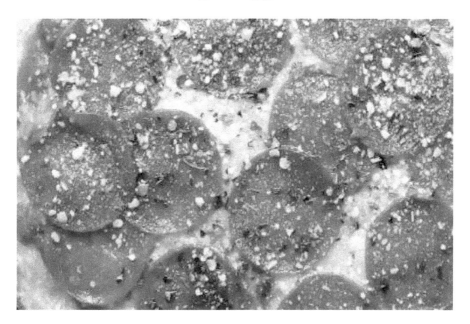

Prep 15 minutes/Cook 30minutes/ Serves 8/ 425°F

Difficulty: Expert

PER SERVING: Calories: 161; Fat: 13g; Saturated Fat: 1g; Carbohydrates: 2g; Protein: 9g; Sodium: 132mg; Fiber: 0g; Sugar: 2g

Ingredients

8 oz. Mozzarella cheese slices full fat

2 tbsp grated parmesan cheese

2 tbsp full-fat cream cheese

1/3 cup almond flour

½ tsp garlic powder

½ tsp salt

2 tbsp whole psyllium husks either whole or ground

Directions

Finely chop and place the mozzarella in a microwaveable container. Cook until melted. (This took about 1.5 minutes.)

Let the cheese cool slightly. Mix with the cream cheese, almond flour, parmesan cheese, garlic powder, and salt. (Knead in with your hands.)

Add the psyllium and shape the dough into a ball and then roll out as flat as you can on parchment paper, pizza stone, or a silicone mat.

Shape the dough as needed and bake at 425°F for about 15-20 minutes.

Flip the crust and bake for about 5 more minutes until browned.

Add the sauce, cheese, and other toppings. Bake for about five more minutes.

Prep 5minutes/ Cook 7 minutes/ Serves 4

Difficulty: Beginner

PER SERVING: Calories: 293; Fat: 3.9g; Saturated Fat: 2g; Protein: 15.6g; Carbohydrates: 1.8g; Sodium: 96mg; Fiber: 0g; Sugar: 1g

Ingredients

1 ¾ cups pre-shredded/grated cheese mozzarella

¾ cup almond flour

2 tbsp full-fat cream cheese

1 medium egg

1 pinch salt

Directions

Mix the shredded cheese, cream cheese, and almond flour in a microwaveable bowl. Microwave using high power for one minute.

Stir and continue cooking on high for another 30 seconds.

Whisk the egg and salt and mix gently with the rest of the fixings.

Roll the dough between two sheets of parchment baking paper. (Don't roll as thin as a thin pizza crust so it can hold the chosen fillings.)

Discard the top baking paper. Slice the dough into squares (the same size as your toasted sandwich maker).

Place one square on the bottom of the sandwich maker, add your choice of fillings.

Place another square of dough on the top and press the lid of the sandwich maker down.

Cook until they're golden brown or about three to five minutes.

Prep 5 minutes/ Cook 7 minutes/ Serves 4

Difficulty: Intermediate

PER SERVING: Calories: 147; Fat: 10g; Saturated Fat: 2g; Protein: 14g; Carbohydrates: 1g; Sodium: 67mg; Fiber: 0g; Sugar: 0g

Ingredients:

1 cup Riced cauliflower - cooked

1 Egg

Spices - optional - ex. parsley, fennel, oregano, etc.

Directions:

Set the oven temperature setting at 450° Fahrenheit.

Spray a 12 " pizza pan with a spritz of cooking oil spray.

Mix the cauliflower, egg, and mozzarella. Press onto the pie plate. Sprinkle with the spices and bake for 12 to 15 minutes. Remove and add the sauce, cheese, and toppings.

Put the pizza under the high-heat broiler to melt the cheese.

Prep 15 minutes/ Cook 30 minutes/ Serves 6/ 350° F

Difficulty: Intermediate

PER SERVING: Calories: 118; Fat: 9g; Saturated Fat: 1g; Protein: 5.6g; Carbohydrates: 1.8g; Sodium: 103mg; Fiber: 0g; Sugar: 4g

Ingredient:

1 cup Almond flour

3 tbsp. Coconut flour

2 tsp. Xanthan gum

1 tsp.Bak. powder

¼ tsp Kosher salt

2 tsp. Apple cider vinegar

1 Egg, lightly beaten

5 tsp. Water

Directions:

Measure out and add the xanthan gum, almond flour, baking powder, coconut flour, and salt to a food processor. Pulse well to fully combine.

With the processor running, add the vinegar, the egg, and water. Add just enough for it to come together into a ball.

Wrap the dough in plastic wrap and knead it through the plastic for a minute or two. Allow the dough to rest for 10 minutes at room temperature for up to five days in the fridge.

If cooking on the stovetop, warm up the skillet using the med-high temperature while your dough rests. For the oven; heat up the baking tray, pizza stone, or skillet to reach 350° Fahrenheit.

Roll out the dough between two sheets of parchment paper. Fold over the edges.

Prepare the pizza crust in the preheated skillet, top-side down first, until blistered (about 2 min.).

Reduce the heat to med-low. Flip the pizza crust, and add the toppings of choice. Cover with a lid.

When ready, serve immediately for best results.

You can store the dough in the refrigerator for approximately five days.

Rolls

Low-carb dinner rolls

Prep 10 minutes/ Cook 10 minutes/ Serves 6/ 350° F

Difficulty: Intermediate

PER SERVING: Calories: 218; Fat: 18g; Saturated Fat: 5g; Protein: 10.7g; Carbohydrates: 5.6g; Sodium: 103mg; Fiber: 3.3g; Sugar: 3g

Ingredients

1 cup almond flour

¼ cup flaxseed (ground)

1 cup Mozzarella (shredded)

1 oz cream cheese

½ tsp baking soda

1 egg

Directions:

Preheat your oven to 400°F.

Using a microwave-safe mixing bowl, put both the mozzarella and cream cheese. Microwave it for one minute. Stir them till they become smooth.

Add eggs in the bowl and stir till they mix well.

In another clean bowl, put your flaxseed, almond flour and baking soda and mix the dry ingredients.

Pour your egg and cheese mix into the bowl with dry ingredients. Use your hand mixer or hands to make dough by kneading.

Slightly wet your hands with coconut oil or olive oil and roll your dough to six balls.

Top them with sesame seeds and place them on the parchment paper.

Bake them for 10 minutes. A golden brown look will indicate that they are done.

Leave them to cool.

Prep 10 minutes/ Cook 20 minutes/ Serves 8/ 350° F

Difficulty: Intermediate

PER SERVING: Calories: 283; Fat: 18g; Saturated Fat: 21g; Protein: 17g; Carbohydrates: 6g; Sodium: 103mg; Fiber: 2g; Sugar: 1g

Ingredients

I/3 cup coconut flour or 1 1/3 cup almond flour

1 ½ cup mozzarella cheese (shredded)

1 ½ tsp baking powder

¼ cup parmesan cheese (grated)

2 ounces cream cheese

2 eggs (large)

Directions:

Preheat your oven to 350°F.

Put your almond flour and baking powder in a clean bowl and mix.

Using another bowl, put your Mozzarella and cream cheese and microwave for a minute. Stir it well after it melts.

Add eggs to the cheese and stir.

Add the egg-cheese mix to the bowl with dry ingredients and mix thoroughly.

Wet your hands and knead dough into a sticky ball.

Put the dough ball on the parchment paper and slice into fourths.

Slice each fourth or quarter into 6 smaller portions.

Roll each small portion into balls.

Roll the balls into the parmesan cheese light for them to coat it.

Grease your 13.75" x 10.5" muffin pan and place 3 dough balls in each cup of the pan.

Prep 10 minutes/ Cook 20 minutes/ Serves 8/ 350° F

Difficulty: Beginner

PER SERVING: Calories: 216; Fat: 16g; Saturated Fat: 4g; Protein: 11g; Carbohydrates: 6g; Sodium: 183mg; Fiber: 2g; Sugar: 1g

Ingredients

1 1/3 cups almond flour

1 ½ cups shredded mozzarella cheese (part skim)

2 oz cream cheese (full fat)

1 ½ tbsp baking powder (aluminum free)

2 tbsps. coconut flour

3 eggs (large)

Directions:

Preheat your oven to 350° F

In a clean bowl, put almond flour, coconut flour and baking powder. Mix well and set it aside.

Using a microwave-safe bowl, put the cream cheese and mozzarella in it and microwave for 30 seconds. Remove the bowl, stir and microwave again for 30 seconds. This should go on until the cheese has entirely melted.

Using a food processor add the cheese, the eggs and flour mix. Process at high speed for uniformity of the dough. (It is normally sticky.)

Knead the dough into a dough ball and separate it into 8 equal pieces. Slightly wet your hands with oil for this step.

Roll each piece with your palms to form a ball and place each ball on the baking sheet. (should be 2 inches apart)

In a bowl, add the remaining egg and whisk. Brush the egg wash on the rolls.

Bake for 20 minutes or until they are golden brown.

Note: The cheese hardens the rolls thus they should be eaten when hot. Microwave them to make soft once they cool.

Keto coconut bread rolls

Prep 10 minutes/ Cook 30 minutes/ Serves 6/ 350° F

Difficulty: Intermediate

PER SERVING: Calories: 172; Fat: 10g; Saturated Fat: 2g; Protein: 10.7g; Carbohydrates: 14g; Sodium: 100mg; Fiber: 9g; Sugar: 1g

Ingredients

½ cup coconut flour

4 tbsps. flaxseed (ground)

2 tbsps. coconut oil

2 tbsps. psyllium husk (powder)

1 tbsp baking powder

1 tbsp apple cider vinegar

¼ cup boiling water

½ tsp salt

2 egg whites

2 eggs (medium size)

Directions:

Preheat your oven to 350°F.

In a mixing bowl, put all your dry ingredients and mix thoroughly. (coconut flour, flaxseed flour, baking powder, psyllium husk powder, salt)

Add eggs and the coconut oil. Blend the ingredients till it resembles breadcrumbs. Pour the apple cider vinegar and mix.

Add the boiling water in bits. (you don't need to use the entire amount) Stir for it to combine well with the mixture.

Line your baking tray with baking paper.

Make 6 divisions of the dough and roll them into balls with your hands.

Place the dough balls on the baking paper.

Bake them for 30 minutes or upon turning to golden brown.

Low carb bread rolls (without eggs)

Prep 15 minutes/ Cook 40 minutes/ Serves 6/ 350° F

Difficulty: Intermediate

PER SERVING: Calories: 230; Fat: 18g; Saturated Fat: 5g; Protein: 6.2g; Carbohydrates: 13.9g; Sodium: 132mg; Fiber: 9.2g; Sugar: 1.9g

Ingredients

¼ cup coconut flour

1 ¼ cup almond flour

¼ cup psyllium husk (ground)

1 cup hot water

1 tbsp olive oil

2 tsp apple cider vinegar

2 tsps. baking powder

½ tsp salt

2 tbsps. sesame seeds (optional)

Directions:

Preheat your oven to 375°F.

Add all your dry ingredients in a bowl. (Coconut flour, almond flour, psyllium powder, baking powder, salt)

Pour the olive oil and apple cider vinegar in the hot water and stir. Thereafter, pour the mix in the bowl and combine thoroughly for a minute. The flour will absorb the water forming the dough. The dough will be soft and sticky. Leave it for 10 minutes for the water mixture to be well absorbed.

Separate the dough into 6 equal portions. Form 6 dough balls as a result.

Line your baking tray with parchment paper.

Place the balls on the baking tray and sprinkle sesame seeds on top. Press the seeds into the dough to prevent falling out.

Bake for 40 minutes at 3750F at the lower section of the oven for the first 30 minutes. Switch them to the top section for the remaining period.

Remove from the oven and let them cool.

Conclusion

Keto friendly, gluten-free breads that you can make and serve for a variety of meals or occasions. As you saw, each of the recipes in this book is incredibly easy to follow, and most of them are also incredibly inexpensive to make.

These breads are made using the normal ingredients you can find locally, so there's no need to have to order anything, or have to go to any specialty stores for any of them. With these breads, you can enjoy the same meals you used to enjoy, but stay on track with your diet as much as you want.

Lose the weight you want to lose, feel great, and still get to indulge in that piping hot piece of bread every now and then. Spread on your favorite topping, and your bread craving will be satisfied.

I hope the recipes in this book were able to inspire you to take your own baking to the next level. As you can see by each of these, you can alter and modify a variety of things to give them that custom spin you need from time to time.

Thanks for downloading this book. It's my firm belief that it has provided you with all the answers to your questions

CPSIA information can be obtained
at www.ICGtesting.com
Printed in the USA
LVHW040450261020
669801LV00004B/258